Exploring God's Decrees, Predestination and Election

PETRUS VAN MASTRICHT

MONERGISM BOOKS

Contents

The Acts and Decrees of God

"According to the purpose of Him who accomplishes all things according to the counsel of His own will." —Ephesians 1:11

Another essential pillar of our faith is the effectiveness of God. I. Our faith, upon which we securely rely for the sustenance of our spiritual lives, stands firmly upon two pillars: the all-encompassing ability of God, through which He can supply us with all that leads to our salvation, and the divine efficacy of God, through which He not only can but indeed does provide. The former, arising from the very essence of God and the existence of distinct divine persons, we have expounded upon thus far. Now, let us explore the latter, and, by way of introduction, contemplate the actions of God in their entirety, including His inner workings and divine decrees. The apostle's teachings in Ephesians 1:11 serve as our guiding light for both of these aspects.

The Guiding Light of Scripture

Rooted in the Holy Word

II. In these verses, the Apostle Paul, with the intent of unveiling the essence of divine actions, illuminates:

A. The very workings of God: "who accomplishes all things." In these words, we discern:

1. The primary agent, concealed behind the particle "of him who...," is undoubtedly God, as we discussed in previous chapters. This may refer either to God in a theological sense, encompassing the entire Trinity, for it is inherent in God, according to each person's unique mode of existence, to bring about all things. Alternatively, it may refer to God in an economic sense, signifying the Father alone, as the one consistently distinguished from the Son throughout the preceding verses. It is in the Son that He brings about all that is necessary for our salvation.

2. The divine action itself: "who accomplishes" (ἐνεργοῦντος). This term signifies an action joined with utmost efficacy, a supreme effectiveness that cannot be constrained. This interpretation is derived from the usage of Scripture. The translators of the Septuagint employ this word in Isaiah 41:4, describing a profoundly efficacious operation that surmounts obstacles, accomplishes its purpose, and removes all hindrances. The Apostle Paul employs the same word in Ephesians 2:2 to express the power of the devil and the dominion of his strength over those who disobey. Consequently, it denotes here an operation of God so potent that no creature's power and no strength of human free will can oppose it. Thus, what comes to pass aligns precisely with His divine purpose.

3. The divine act itself: "all things" (τὰ πάντα). This encompasses either (1) a comprehensive and all-encompassing "all things" without exception, including not only the blessings of grace but also everything else. This includes not only virtuous deeds but also deeds that might appear as evil, albeit not morally evil. For God masterfully directs even such actions toward His ultimate purpose. This argument proceeds from the lesser to

the greater: if God governs all things, even the most minor creations, then how much more does He orchestrate events crucial to human salvation? Or (2) a narrower interpretation, signifying "all these things," specifically referring to matters concerning our redemption, which have been the constant theme of his discourse. Or (3) an even narrower view, focusing on those deeds exclusive to God, such as sending Christ on His divine mission, raising Him from the dead, revealing the fulfillment of the gospel, and its dependence upon Him. However, it is vital to note that not only does this encompass the works of the entire Trinity, but it also includes the economic works of the Father, in His role as the first person, eternally devising the plan of redemption and subsequently bringing it to fruition in time.

The Divine Guidance

The Standard of His Work: "According to the counsel of His own will" (Ephesians 1:11). The eternal covenant of peace between the Father and the Son serves as the guiding principle for the entire mission of redemption. It is crucial to note:

1. The Divine Purpose: "According to the purpose" (κατὰ τὴν πρόθεσιν). In Scripture, "purpose" (πρόθεσις) sometimes signifies the entirety of the election decree or the covenant of peace. At other times, it refers to the initial act of election, wherein God purposed to manifest the glory of His mercy through the free blessing of specific individuals, whom He designated as vessels for His blessings. And yet, at times, it denotes the third act of election, wherein God intends to prepare the means conducive to this blessing. Therefore, election is sometimes described as being in accordance with His purpose (Ephesians 1:11), and at other times, His purpose aligns with election (Romans 9:11). Additionally, election occurs according to the purpose, counsel, and good pleasure of God's will (Ephesians 1:5).

2. The Divine Counsel: "According to the counsel" (κατὰ τὴν βουλήν). Within any counsel, apart from the purpose of the end, there lies deliberation concerning the means and a particular intention regarding those means, while rejecting all others. While God is not subject to deliberation as it implies ignorance, such terminology is attributed to God due to the certainty of His knowledge, His wisdom, and His perfectly ordered methodology. This methodology springs freely from His choice, rational approval, and divine satisfaction, rather than from His nature.

3. The Intention of His Will: "Of His will" (τοῦ θελήματος). Here, the chosen means are applied, freely yet wisely and justly, since they derive from the counsel of His will and His absolute authority over all creation. In this passage, the general approach of all divine operations is initially revealed, followed by specific insights into the divine decrees, which we will explore further in the subsequent sections of this chapter.

FIRST THEOREM—Divine Activity
The Doctrinal Aspect
The Divine Hand in All

III. It is abundantly evident from the text that God is the ultimate source of all actions (Ephesians 1:23). Consequently, all things are attributed to originate from Him, flow through Him, and ultimately lead back to Him (Romans 11:36). Even the Savior affirms that the Father is ceaselessly at work, and likewise, He Himself is engaged in divine labor (John 5:17). This truth stands as clear as day for all to behold, for God is the prime mover of all things, without whom no action in the world could ever come to pass. For if the primary cause remains inert, how could any secondary cause possibly act? It goes without saying that activity is inherently more perfect than inactivity. Therefore, it is entirely befitting for the Most Perfect One to be ceaselessly engaged in action.

The Divine Nature of Action

IV. Furthermore, the concepts of working, acting, and effecting, at least in the realm of created beings, encompass four essential elements: (1) the agent, within whom resides (2) the capacity or power to act, leading to (3) the actual action or operation, which results in (4) the final work or outcome. In created beings, these four elements are distinct, yet in God, the embodiment of pure, unadulterated action, they are inseparable and one and the same. In God, there is nothing but His very essence in action. It is worth noting that even though, in His external works, the work itself differs from the One who works and the act of working, here, divine activity encompasses two essential aspects: the active essence of God and its relationship to the work at hand. In the works of created beings, both the agent and the work transition from potentiality to actuality. The one who works, previously only possessing the potential to act, now actualizes that potential. Simultaneously, the work, formerly a potential outcome, manifests in actuality. However, in divine works, only the work itself undergoes this transition, as it is brought under the sway of the unchanging and ever-active divine essence. In God, no alteration from potentiality to actuality occurs due to His ceaseless activity.

The All-Encompassing Divine Work

V. Furthermore, it is essential to understand that God's work extends to all things (Romans 11:36)—to every entity possessing essence and goodness, whether in the realm of nature or morality. The operation of all secondary causes undeniably hinges upon the operation of the primary cause, which is absolute and supreme. This dependence is true not only concerning the essence of the work itself but also regarding all its inherent aspects. As it is written, "I, Jehovah, do all these things" (Isaiah 45:7; Lamentations 3:37–38). Consequently, God does not, and indeed cannot, bring about morally evil things or sins, for they are not effects but rather deficiencies in the effects. Nor can God transgress the law, as the essence of this evil solely lies in such transgressions (1 John 3:4).

The Unique Workings of the Divine Persons

VI. The works of God, specifically His external works, can be contemplated in two dimensions: firstly, as they emanate from His essence and omnipotence, which are intrinsically linked, as we have previously elucidated; secondly, as they stem from the divine persons. In the latter aspect, we find (1) a cooperative effort among the persons, as they all work inseparably towards the same goal (John 5:17, 19). As the adage goes, the works of God ad extra are indivisible (John 16:13–14). Therefore, (a) each person operates "a se," from Himself, with regard to the power that is at work (John 5:26). There exists one shared power of operation. Consequently, (b) in these works, there is no hierarchy among the persons, for all act in unison through the same power (John 5:21–23). Additionally, (2) there is a distinct mode of operation for each person, as each operates in accordance with their particular mode of subsistence: the Father acts from Himself, through the Son and the Holy Spirit; the Son acts from the Father, through the Holy Spirit; and the Holy Spirit acts from the Father and the Son, through Himself, as expounded in our chapter on the Trinity. Furthermore, (3) there is an appropriation, whereby a work that is common to all three persons is attributed to one for a specific reason. Thus, the first person is credited with the initial external work, creation, and the preliminary plan of redemption through predestination. The second person assumes responsibility for redemption, having achieved it through His own blood. Lastly, the third person is particularly associated with sanctification and its related aspects, as He is immediately involved in this process. Lastly, (4) there is a unique termination of operation, whereby the final phase of a work shared by all persons is specifically associated with one person. For example, the conclusion of the active incarnation, a work common to all three persons, specifically pertains to the second person who undertakes it by assuming human nature.

The Distribution of Divine Works

VII. Theologians conventionally categorize divine works into two distinct realms: internal or immanent works, wherein nothing emerges beyond God or distinct from God, and external or transient works, wherein something distinct from God comes into existence. Within the former category, we find either personal and characteristic works, which serve to distinguish the divine persons from each other. These include begetting, exclusively attributed to the Father (Psalm 2:7); being begotten, or the manner of proceeding as one begotten, which belongs to the Son (Micah 5:1); and proceeding as one spirated, ascribed to the Holy Spirit (John 15:26). Alternatively, there are essential works that convey the persons toward one another and toward creatures. For instance, the Father's knowledge, love, and glorification of the Son, reciprocated by the Son toward the Father. Moreover, these essential works extend toward creatures as God's knowledge, love, election, and reprobation of His creation, prominently encompassing the divine decrees. The latter category, external works, pertains to creation and providence.

The Instructive Aspect

Four Debates Concerning God's Works

VIII. Firstly, we encounter the Epicureans who effectively deny that God is actively involved in all things. Their belief portrays Him as distant and uninvolved, maintaining indifference towards the world's affairs. According to their view, the intricate work of creating, sustaining, and governing countless creatures does not disrupt His tranquility and blessedness. Yet, they underestimate the truth found in Isaiah 40:28, "The everlasting God, the Lord who creates the ends of the earth, will not grow tired or weary." Secondly, the Stoics reject this truth by placing God's works under the dominion of fate or the causality of secondary forces. They imply that God neither orchestrates this causal interplay nor possesses the power to alter it as He pleases. Thirdly, the Pelagians deny it by excluding God's active involvement in the initial determination of free choice and even in the existence of sin, both in terms of its lawlessness and its underlying foundation. We will address these issues in their respective contexts, particularly when discussing divine providence. Fourthly, the Socinians and Vorstius dismiss this truth by attributing accidental works to God, separate from His essence. However, their views are contradicted by the doctrines of God's simplicity and immutability, as we shall explain in their appropriate contexts.

The Practical Aspect

The Efficacy of God: 1. Revealing His Glory

IX. The fact that God works in all things primarily serves to manifest His glory, as it is from Him, through Him, and to Him that all things exist, resulting in eternal praise (Romans 11:36). He is the Creator of light and the Author of darkness, identified as Jehovah, the One who orchestrates all these wonders (Isaiah 45:7). This revelation magnifies the glory of: (1) His self-sufficiency, for the One who works in all things remains unaffected by external influences (Romans 11:35); (2) His omnipotence, as He, unaltered by external forces, accomplishes His every desire (Psalm 115:3); (3) His wisdom, for all His works are executed with wisdom (Psalm 119:24); (4) His grace, as He is the source of all goodness that humanity enjoys from creation. He is the One who actively works in all things and specifically within us, both to desire and to act (Philippians 2:13). It is by His grace alone that we are what we are and can become all that we can be. His grace within us is not in vain (1 Corinthians 15:10).

1. A Reproof of Impiety

X. Secondly, it serves as a stern reproof to those who harbor atheistic beliefs, asserting that God is inactive, that neither good nor evil emanates from the mouth of the Most High (Lamentations 3:37–38). These individuals, who murmur in their hearts, claiming, "Jehovah does not perform good, nor does He perpetrate evil" (Zephaniah 1:12), fail to love God or seek Him, as if He were incapable of bestowing goodness upon them. They cynically declare, "Worshipping God is in vain; what advantage is it to keep His commandments?" (Malachi 3:14). They neither revere nor fear Him, as if He were impotent to visit them with calamity (Psalms 10:6, 11; 119:7, 10). In their folly, they fashion a senseless idol out of the God who actively operates in all things.

1. A Source of Comfort in Adverse Times

XI. Thirdly, it offers solace to the righteous amidst adversity, assuring them that God is the Creator of both light and darkness, the One who forges peace and fashions calamity (Isaiah 45:7). They find solace in the knowledge that He is their God. Recognizing that no misfortune befalls a city without the Lord's consent (Amos 3:6), they remain silent and uncomplaining during trials, acknowledging that the Lord is the orchestrator of their tribulations (Psalms 39:9).

1. Nurturing and Fortifying Faith

XII. Fourthly, it nurtures and strengthens our faith in God, compelling us to entrust our paths to Jehovah, for He will accomplish His purposes (Psalms 37:5). In all circumstances, we rely solely on Him, recognizing that without Him, neither good nor ill can befall us.

1. Binding Us to God and Godliness

XIII. Fifthly, it binds us to God, prompting us to adhere to Him with genuine reverence and godliness. We refuse to be estranged from Him, whether due to hope in any goodness or fear of any harm that may come from creatures apart from God. Knowing that God actively works in all things, we strive to keep Him continually at our right hand, never departing from His presence (Psalms 16:8). If God is on our side, who or what could be against us (Romans 8:31)? Conversely, if He is opposed to us, who or what could possibly support us? After all, He orchestrates all things in all things. While we have briefly touched upon these matters here, they may be explored in greater depth in another context, particularly within the chapter on divine providence.

The SECOND THEOREM—The Decrees of God His Internal Workings

The Doctrinal Aspect

XIV. Within the divine actions, which we have thus far discussed in a general sense, we first encounter God's internal operations, particularly His decrees. Through these decrees, He is said to bring about all things according to His will. Indeed, both testaments affirm the concept of decrees in relation to God. For instance, we find in Isaiah 14:26–27, "This is the counsel that has been counseled by me... Jehovah God of hosts has decreed" (similarly, see Daniel 4:24; Psalms 2:7; Zephaniah 2:2; Acts 2:23; 4:28; Romans 8:29–30; Matthew 11:26, among others). Because God does not act by mere instinct or without reason, but rather by choice and counsel, especially considering that He possesses intellect and will, as we have previously demonstrated and as is universally acknowledged. It is evident that acting from counsel is a greater perfection than acting from mere nature or instinct. While the term "decree" may not be explicitly used in Scripture, the concept is undeniably present, conveyed through various synonyms, as we will illustrate in the subsequent section. Therefore, we should not deny that decrees are rightfully attributed to God, as both intellect and will are His exclusive attributes, and He acts freely and in accordance with rational pleasure, as we have previously argued. It is worth noting that the necessity for deliberation and the presence of ignorance, which are characteristic of creaturely decrees and counsels, do not apply to God's decrees. These limitations pertain solely to the realm of created beings, and they should be removed from our understanding of God, as we typically do when discussing God's communicable attributes.

Is a Decree a Definite Pronouncement of God?

XV. A decree typically signifies a specific pronouncement, whether it be from a judge when rendering a verdict among disputing parties or any other determination made following careful consideration. It is referred to by various names such as counsel, good pleasure, purpose, προορισμένη βουλή ("predetermined plan" - Acts 2:23; 4:28; Ephesians 1:9, 11), and also "(□□decree" - Psalms 2:7). In the context of God, a decree represents nothing other than His predetermined pronouncement regarding the ordering of all future events according to the counsel of His will. It encompasses a specific pronouncement involving three aspects: (1) the act of decreeing, which is essentially the very nature of God, considered in the manner of a vital action – the decreeing God Himself; (2) His inclination and relationship toward an object to be realized in time, without any alteration in God or enhancement of His essence, as this inclination is not something additional to His essence that would perfect it further. In this sense, the decree differs from His essence, as the essence does not entail any inclination or relationship. (3) The thing decreed, or to be actualized in time, which is truly distinct from God. Concerning the first aspect, God's decree is one, necessary, and eternal; regarding the second, the inclination is free and multifaceted, akin to a circle with one center and various radii extending from it, yet never conflicting with it.

The Definite Pronouncement of a Decree Encompasses Three Aspects

XVI. Moreover, this specific pronouncement of a decree involves: (1) an ultimate purpose set before the One decreeing, which, for God, is exclusively His own glory. For this reason, He is said to work all things for Himself (Proverbs 16:4) and unto Himself (Romans 11:36). (2) A consideration of the means, which, in the case of creatures, entails deliberation to choose and employ the most suitable and effective means. This is why a decree is often referred to as a counsel. (3) An intention of the will, by which the chosen means, selected from many, is directed towards its intended objective. This intention indeed stands as the cause of all futurity but not of the future thing itself, whether it be good or evil. This is because the decree is an internal action that produces nothing outside of God, and futurity has existed eternally, while the future thing comes into being in time.

The Decree Concerns the Determination of Futurity

XVII. Thus, this specific pronouncement of God concerns the individual futurity of all things, whether they are necessary, contingent, free, good, or evil. Nonetheless, the future things themselves do not receive that pronouncement as their cause. Hence, the decree is indeed the cause of the futurity of sin, but not of the future sin itself, which finds its cause in the free choice of the one committing the sin. For if the cause of futurity were not God's decree, then that thing would have been future from eternity by its own inherent nature, which would imply a form of fate more extreme than that of the Stoics. It is evident that by this logic, something that will exist in time would be the cause of that which has existed eternally, effectively positioning an effect before its own cause. Nevertheless, a future thing ultimately follows the decree either by creation or providence as its cause if it is good, or only as its precursor if it is evil.

And this Futurity is to be Brought About Either by Accomplishing or by Allowing

XVIII. Consequently, God intends to bring about the future and future events according to the decree, either by bringing them into fruition if they are good, or by allowing them effectively if they are evil. This leads to a division of the decree into two categories: one that brings about the decree and one that permits it.

The Guiding Principle for Bringing About the Decree is His Counsel

XIX. Ultimately, the guiding principle, or that which resembles a guiding principle, for implementing this decree is the counsel of His will, more precisely (Ephesians 1:11). However, counsel does not pertain to

God in the same way it does to creatures concerning deliberation, which presupposes ignorance to be dispelled through deliberation. Instead, counsel pertains to God with the attributes of perfect judgment, akin to the judgment that often follows deliberate consideration in creatures. This judgment in God excludes recklessness and wisely and fittingly prepares all things, which is why it is called ,□□□meaning "undertaking" or "devising" (Proverbs 8:22; Isaiah 5:12).

The Characteristics of God's Decree: It is Eternal

XX. Furthermore, this decree of God is, firstly, eternal (Ephesians 1:4). This is why all His works are said to be known to God from ancient times (Acts 15:18), and the purpose for which grace is bestowed upon us is said to have existed from before eternal times (2 Timothy 1:9). Scripture also speaks of God predestining His wisdom in a mystery before the ages (1 Corinthians 2:7), not just concerning the act of decreeing, but also regarding His inclination toward the future event to be realized. Otherwise, by decreeing, God would transition from potentiality to actuality and be susceptible to change, which Scripture explicitly refutes (Malachi 3:6; James 1:17).

It is Also Most Free

XXI. Furthermore, the second characteristic of God's decree is its freedom, and it is the utmost freedom (Romans 9:11; Jeremiah 18:6; Matthew 11:26; 20:15). It's not because God could exist without the ability or act of decreeing, as that would mean He could exist without intellect and will. It's also not because the ability or act of decreeing could exist without a tendency toward some object, as then there would be a decree without a decree. And it's certainly not because God has ever been indifferent to decreeing or not decreeing, as that would mean the decree is not eternal and God could change through decreeing. The decree is free because: (1) God, by nature, is indifferent to decreeing in one way or another; (2) when decreeing in one way and not another, God is determined by nothing but His own reasons, which is rational complacency. The decree of God is not just free, like a decree of creatures, even though it is determined by the supreme cause. It is most free, or absolutely free, because God is entirely independent.

It is Most Wise

XXII. The third characteristic of God's decree is its supreme wisdom. In contemplating this, we are inclined to exclaim, "O the depths of the riches both of the wisdom and knowledge of God!" (Romans 11:33–34; Psalms 104:24). God chooses and arranges the means that are most fitting for His ends (Romans 8:28–30). God does not decree anything without reason, for even though the divine decree excludes all causes that would produce it, it undeniably requires reasons (most of which are concealed from us but are fully known to Him) because it is profoundly wise.

It is Absolute and Immutable

XXIII. Finally, the fourth characteristic of God's decree is its absoluteness and immutability (Isaiah 46:10; Acts 4:28; Proverbs 19:21). Although the decree is often dependent on certain causes and conditions, the act of decreeing itself remains entirely independent of every cause and condition, thus making it absolutely unchanging.

It Has Universal Effectiveness

XXIV. Fifth, the decree of God is marked by its universal effectiveness (Psalm 115:3; 135:6; Isaiah 14:24). While it doesn't directly cause the thing decreed, such as sin, it does affect the certainty of the event, not imposing necessity on things but ensuring their occurrence. It doesn't prevent events from arising due to proximate contingent causes that aren't predetermined for those outcomes. Nor does it infringe upon our free will since it doesn't hinder our choices. Rather than forcing all things by hard necessity, the divine decree serves as the source of all contingency. Without God or some supreme, entirely free divinity that assigns and connects contingent causes to their outcomes, there would be no contingency at all.

The Object of the Divine Decree

XXV. The object preceding the decree is a possible thing, while the object finalizing the decree is a future thing. God decrees specific future outcomes from these possible things. The decree encompasses all future events, even particular sins, as we mentioned earlier. Although the sin itself results from a transgression of the law, its future occurrence stems solely from the divine decree.

The Decree is Singular in the Decreeing Act

XXVI. God's decree is singular and profoundly simple when it comes to the act of decreeing. God, in one eternal moment without deliberation, determined all future things that have been, are, and will be. However, it appears manifold and diverse in its tendency towards various objects, resulting in various terminations and relations. This is why terms like "counsels" (Isaiah 25:1), "thoughts" (Isaiah 55:8), and "works" (Proverbs 8:22) are mentioned in Scripture concerning God's decree. While there are many decrees, they coexist in a beautifully ordered and wise harmony. We conceive this order not because there are distinct acts of decreeing, or one act that is subsequent to another in time or nature, but because we perceive different facets, so to speak, of the same divine counsel. We connect them in an orderly manner to better understand and fully appreciate the wisdom within the decree. It's neither proper nor fitting for God to decree one thing without another, such as creating the human race without a plan for His own glorification. We distinguish different aspects of the decree and call one part or decree the reason, if not the productive cause, of another. We draw connections and reasoning from one to another, as the apostle Paul also exemplified (Romans 8:32, 29–30).

The Divine Order in the Decrees

Through this order in the divine decrees, we understand that God wills the end before the means to that end, and among the means, those that are closer to the end come first. Thus, what is initially intended is realized last in execution, according to the order of intention. In terms of execution, however, God wills the means before the end. It's important to note that this doesn't imply different volitions within God, where one is prior to another or one causes another. Rather, it pertains to what is decreed and willed by God. With God, there exists a volition and wise coordination of what is prior and what is posterior, especially concerning the means and the end, which He has connected in a suitable and free manner. Nevertheless, neither God nor His decree depends on anything, condition, or means. As we've mentioned before, just as God's decree is one, it is exceedingly absolute, even though the execution can be conditioned, as can the effect and production. However, all of these depend on the one absolute decree.

The Nature of the Decree: Effecting and Permitting

XXVII. The divine decree is divided into two categories: the effecting decree and the permitting decree. This division is not due to the decree itself being an effective cause, as it is an immanent action within God. Rather, it reflects God's decision in time to effect some things and permit others. The effecting decree encompasses all things that are good, both natural and moral since God is the primary and universal cause of all existence. The permitting decree, on the other hand, pertains solely to the procurement of futurity, where the future events result from the creature's action with God not actively preventing them. This latter decree specifically concerns moral evil or sin, which God does not actively cause but allows to occur (Acts 2:23–24; 4:27–28).

The Elenctic Part

Addressing a Fundamental Question: Is the Divine Decree God's Essence?

XXVIII. Let us explore a profound question: Is the decree of God identical to His very essence? This matter has elicited varying opinions throughout history. Among the Greeks, there was a debate on whether God's essence and His will were one and the same. Some affirmed this, as seen in the writings of Justin Martyr or the author of the book "Questions for the Greeks," while others denied it. The subsequent Church fathers, especially Augustine in his work "On the Essence of God," as well as Scholastic theologians like John of Damascus, Peter Lombard, and Thomas Aquinas, affirmed that God's essence and His will were indeed identical. However, in more recent times, Remonstrant Apologists, aiming to find favor with Socinians and to challenge the simplicity of God and the immutability of His decrees, denied this identity. The Socinians, taking a more explicit stance, rejected it and introduced the notion of accidents in God, seeking to undermine His simplicity and immutability. On the other hand, the Reformed tradition maintained that the things decreed by God were essentially distinct from His divine essence. They also acknowledged that while the tendency of the decree toward a particular object was not the very essence of God, it was an indispensable component for the formulation of the decree. Without this tendency, there would be a decree that decreed nothing. However, concerning the act of decreeing itself, they held that it was synonymous with the divine essence, except that, when considered absolutely and in itself, the essence did not encompass the tendency toward this or that object, which was formally implied by the decree. It is important to note that among the Reformed, there were those who made distinctions between the essence and the decree, but in a way that did not allow for any composition in God. This was because the tendency was merely a relation, which, strictly speaking, had no existence that could render God composite.

The Reasons Behind This Position

The Reformed theologians argued that the decree was indeed the same as the essence of God for several reasons:

1. Divine Simplicity: God's divine simplicity implies the rejection of all accidents, as previously demonstrated in our discussion of the simplicity of God.

2. Divine Infinity: God's infinity does not permit distinctions, parts, or any form of composition, as we discussed in an earlier section.

3. Identity with God's Intellect and Will: The decree in God is nothing other than His intellect and will, which undoubtedly coincide with His essence.

4. Rejection of Imperfection: Accidents, by their very nature, suggest imperfection, and such imperfections are incongruent with the nature of the Most Perfect One.

Objections Addressed

It is important to respond to objections raised against the idea that the decree of God is synonymous with His essence:

1. Objection: Some argue that there are many decrees in God, whereas the essence is only one. If by "decrees" we mean the things decreed, then indeed there are many, and they are distinct from God's essence and from each other. If, however, we refer to the tendency toward objects, which results in multiple decrees, this is not something separate from the essence but a mere relation. It distinguishes between decrees but does not introduce composition. Moreover, if by "decrees" we refer to the decreeing act, it is nothing other than the essence of God as far as we conceive it to be actively involved in determining the future of things.

2. Objection: It is suggested that the decrees in God are free, while the essence is necessary. However, the act of decreeing does not exist freely but necessarily in God, just as the capacity to decree exists necessarily in rational creatures. The tendency of this act toward a specific object is not free but necessary, as there must be something to decree. However, the freedom lies in the

selection of one object over another. It's crucial to note that we do not regard this tendency as the essence of God but only as the act of decreeing, conceived by us in relation to the thing being decreed or the act of decreeing itself.

The Question of the Eternality of God's Decrees

Now, let us address another significant question: Are all the decrees of God eternal? This inquiry has given rise to differing viewpoints among various theological traditions.

The Perspective of Our Adversaries

Secondly, it is important to consider whether all the decrees of God are eternal. The Pelagians, Socinians, and Remonstrants, in order to maintain certain positions, assert that not all divine decrees are eternal. They do so to safeguard the ideas that (1) the decrees of God are not identical to God Himself, (2) human free choice consists of independent indifference, which could be compromised by the eternity of divine decrees, and (3) some decrees are established daily in accordance with human choice. While they concede that certain divine decrees, such as those pertaining to the creation, preservation, and governance of the world, as well as the sending of Christ into the world and the granting of eternal salvation to the obedient, have existed eternally and do not affect the indifference of free choice, they deny that all divine decrees share this eternal character.

The Perspective of the Reformed with Their Reasons

On the contrary, the Reformed perspective affirms that each and every decree of God is indeed eternal. They hold this view for several reasons:

1. As mentioned earlier, according to the Reformed belief, the decrees of God are inseparable from God Himself. Consequently, if God is eternal, His decrees must also be eternal.

2. From all eternity, God possesses foreknowledge of all future events (Acts 15:18), and this foreknowledge is intricately con-

nected to His decrees. It would be impossible for God to possess this foreknowledge without His eternal decrees.

3. By contrast, if we were to accept the opposing viewpoint, it would imply that from eternity up to the point of decreeing in time, God would have been ignorant, lacking in understanding, and uncertain about many events that would come to pass.

4. Furthermore, God would only acquire, and continue to acquire, most of His perfections related to knowledge of things not decreed from eternity, which would mean that He would not have been most perfect from eternity and thus could not truly be God.

5. Our adversaries, by adopting their opposing view, inadvertently establish a form of necessity even more rigid than Stoicism. If events that are currently unfolding in time were predetermined to be future from eternity and this futurity is not dependent on God's free decree, then it could only be dependent on the events themselves. Consequently, if these events were deemed future from eternity without any decree, not even God Himself could have ordained anything different from them, effectively making God subject to the predetermined futurity of these events.

Counterarguments

If they should raise objections to the contrary, I offer the following responses:

1. Objection: God alone is eternal, but the decrees are not God; therefore, they are not eternal.

   ○ Response: (a) We have already demonstrated in the previous section that the decrees are, in fact, God Himself, and how this is so. (b) Our adversaries themselves acknowledge that certain decrees of God are from eternity, so at least some decrees are God Himself. Why not consider all of them as such? (c) The apostle, in Ephesians 3:11, states that despite the fact that the decrees were made, they are still eternal: "according to the eternal purpose, which he made." Therefore, "which he made" is synonymous with "which he conceived."

2. Objection: Because the decrees of God are free, they cannot be eternal.

   ◦ Response: (a) According to the confession of our adversaries, some decrees of God are indeed from eternity. Therefore, eternity is not incompatible with freedom, or not all decrees of God would be considered free. (b) They are free in the sense that they do not arise from a necessity of the divine nature but from rational complacency. Such a nature of the decrees being from eternity does not contradict their freedom. (c) They are free concerning their determined tendency toward a particular object, not in terms of the act of decreeing itself.

3. Objection: There is no contingent or voluntary effect from eternity, but the decrees of God are contingent and voluntary effects. Every such effect is posterior to its cause.

   ◦ Response: (a) A decree, when referring to the thing decreed, is indeed posterior to its cause and, therefore, not eternal. However, a decree, in the context of the decreeing act, is not posterior to the thing decreed but coexists with the decreeing act. (b) The posteriority of a decree is only in the order of nature, not in the order of time, just as rays are posterior to the sun in the order of nature but coexist with it in time.

4. Objection: Some decrees are posterior to others, indicating not all decrees are eternal, as there is no prior and posterior in eternity.

○ Response: (a) Prior and posterior decrees exist only when considering the thing decreed, not when focusing on the decreeing act itself. God decreed all things through a single and most simple act. (b) Prior and posterior decrees are a result of our manner of conceiving them, but not inherent in the decrees themselves. (c) There are decrees that are conceptually prior and posterior to each other in the order of nature, but not in the order of time.

5. Objection: Certain decrees of God occur in time, so not all decrees are from eternity. This is evident from Jeremiah 18:11, 31:28, and Deuteronomy 28:63.

○ Response: These texts do not pertain to decrees but rather to promises and threats, which are distinct from decrees in their nature and purpose.

Conditioned Decrees

The question arises: Are there conditioned decrees of God? On this matter, there are differences of opinion.

Pelagians, Pelagianizers, Socinians, Arminians, papists, Lutherans, and those outside the Reformed Church argue in favor of conditioned decrees. They propose the existence of antecedent and consequent decrees, where God determined to save each and every person if they choose to believe and repent.

The Reformed perspective, however, distinguishes between two aspects: the thing decreed and the decreeing act of God. They acknowledge the presence of conditioned decrees regarding the thing decreed. In this sense, God from eternity willed that certain events would occur based on prior conditions, such as an individual's salvation being contingent on their faith and repentance. However, they firmly deny that the decreeing act of God depends on any condition.

Here are the reasons for this Reformed stance:

1. The decree of God represents His will, as stated in Ephesians 1:11, "according to the counsel of His will." However, it has already been established that there is no conditioned will in God.

2. As discussed earlier, the decree of God is God Himself. Therefore, if God is not dependent on a condition, neither is His decree.

3. The first and independent being, which God is, cannot be subject to dependency without contradiction. Consequently, His decree cannot be subject to conditions.

4. A decree existing from eternity, as demonstrated earlier, cannot be contingent on conditions that arise in time.

5. A conditioned decree, due to its dependence on conditions, would imply a temporal origin, contrary to the eternal nature of God.

6. God would not be able to foreknow and predict events dependent on human free will if His knowledge were contingent on conditional decrees. Such a scenario would introduce ignorance and imperfection in God.

7. In God, all things are absolute, as affirmed in passages like Psalms 115:3, Isaiah 46:10, and Job 42:2.

An Objection Addressed

Now, it is important to address an objection that may arise. Some argue to the contrary, suggesting that the divine decree can be changed and suspended upon conditions supplied by creatures, citing Jeremiah 18:7–10 as an example. However, it is essential to clarify that it is not the decree itself that changes or is suspended upon a condition when God promises something good or threatens something evil. Rather, it is the outcome or the thing decreed that is affected by such conditions. It should be noted that the decree and promises are fundamentally different, with the decree being eternal and the promises being temporal. Therefore, while the promises may be subject to conditions and change due to them, the decrees are not immediately suspended upon conditions or altered in the same manner.

1. Is There a Decree Congruent to Circumstances?

Now, let us consider the question of whether there is a decree congruent to circumstances.

The Remonstrants and Jesuits, in an attempt to navigate the matter of conversion while not entirely excluding the role of divine decree and grace, propose that among humans, some individuals possess a nature more inclined to conversion than others. According to their perspective, if such a person is called in a manner that aligns with their nature, considering factors like timing, location, and motives, they will respond to this congruent calling. They argue that, through the strength of their free choice, these individuals will freely convert themselves and determine themselves toward faith and repentance. Furthermore, they assert that God has decreed to call these individuals in a manner that is congruent with their nature.

The Reformed Perspective and Its Reasons

In contrast to the aforementioned view, the Reformed perspective asserts that all human beings, due to the fall, are equally spiritually dead and incapable of belief, regardless of the circumstances of their calling. They argue against the congruent decree for several reasons:

1. Scriptural Teaching: As previously mentioned, the Scriptures teach that all individuals are spiritually dead in sin (Ephesians 2:1–3), rendering them equally incapable of any spiritual goodness, including the simplest of righteous thoughts (1 Corinthians 2:14; 2 Corinthians 3:5; Romans 8:7–8; Titus 3:3; Jeremiah 13:23; Genesis 6:5; 8:21, among others).

2. Priority of the Decree: Scripture indicates that the divine decree precedes both circumstances and conversion (Acts 13:48; Romans 8:29–30).

3. Role of Grace: The same Scripture attributes the determination of the will toward conversion solely to the efficacious work of divine grace, effectively bending the will (Philippians 2:12–13; Proverbs 21:1; Romans 15:18; 1 Corinthians 15:10).

4. Dependency on Circumstances: The congruent decree, by making God coincide with His own decree, renders the independent and inherently first God dependent and subservient to suitable and congruent circumstances, effectively molding His decree to fit them.

5. Connection and Fate: This decree establishes a connection, even an inseparable one, between congruent circumstances and events like Peter's spontaneous conversion. Paradoxically, while attempting to avoid the necessity arising from an absolute decree, proponents of this view inadvertently embrace a fate more rigid than Stoicism.

6. Uncertain Connection: Alternatively, it presupposes an uncertain connection that God could not foresee with certainty,

thereby undermining God's omniscience. What lacks certainty cannot be foreknown with absolute certainty.

7. Independent Attribution: The congruent decree attributes conversion and faith independently to human choice, making both God and these outcomes dependent on human decisions.

The Foundation of Our Adversaries' Opinion

The primary basis for our adversaries' position is the belief that a congruent decree preserves human free choice. However, we contend that they mistakenly assume that human liberty rests on sheer independent indifference. In reality, true liberty lies in the ability to act based on rational complacency, which the absolute decree of God neither negates nor undermines, especially since God decreed from eternity that individuals like Peter would freely believe and repent out of His divine counsel.

The Question of an Antecedent and General Decree

Now, let us consider the fifth question: Is there an antecedent and consequent, general and special decree of God? The Remonstrants and Jesuits, in their pursuit of promoting independently indifferent human choice and advocating for a general predestination, election, and reprobation that focus more on the state of individuals than on their specific identities, propose the existence of an antecedent and general decree. According to this view, God established a general decree, for instance, decreeing that all who believe will be saved, followed by a subsequent and special decree that ensures salvation for an individual like Peter, who chooses to believe.

Arguments Presented by the Reformed

However, the Reformed position does not endorse the notion of an antecedent and general decree, citing several reasons:

1. Limits of General Knowledge: General knowledge arises through discursive reasoning and abstraction from specific instances. This form of reasoning implies a dependence on par-

ticulars and, to some extent, ignorance, as it involves acquiring knowledge not previously possessed.

2. Redundancy: A general decree is considered superfluous because it presupposes the existence of a subsequent, distinct, and special decree that both restricts and effectively supersedes it.

3. Redundancy: A general decree is considered superfluous because a special decree, which accounts for each and every individual matter, eliminates the need for a general concept. God, who knows all things through a single, most simple act, does not require a general decree.

4. Incongruity with God's Nature: Assigning God a general decree is inconsistent with His infinite perfection since nothing in God is general, indeterminate, or dependent on other things or individual matters.

5. Unworthiness of God: Such a decree would be unworthy of God, as it implies that God decrees, through an antecedent and general decree, salvation for every individual, despite His eternal foreknowledge that this will never come to pass.

Objection

If someone objects by referencing passages of Scripture, such as John 3:16, "That whoever believes should not perish but have eternal life," or Acts 10:43, "That whoever believes in him has forgiveness of sins through his name," it is essential to understand that these passages do not pertain to decrees but rather to general promises and threats. God uses these general terms to communicate with humanity, accommodating the limitations of individuals who may struggle to comprehend specific details.

The Question of a Mutable Decree

Let us now consider the sixth question: Is there a mutable decree of God? The Socinians, Arminians, Jesuits, Lutherans, and other proponents of Pelagian doctrines, motivated by their belief in a changeable free will that can shift from one state to another in a matter of hours, and also because they teach that conditioned, universal election can transform into reprobation due to unfulfilled conditions, propose the existence of mutable decrees.

Reasons Presented by the Reformed

The Reformed, however, assert that every decree of God is immutable, offering the following reasons:

1. Immutability of God: Every decree of God is synonymous with God Himself, as explained in §XXVIII. Therefore, if God is unchangeable, His decrees are likewise unchangeable.

2. Eternality of Decrees: As previously established in §XXIX, every decree of God is eternal, and in eternity, there is no fluctuation or change.

3. God as the First Being: If God were subject to change initiated by something external to Him, He would no longer be the first and most supreme being.

4. Nature of Change: Any change in God would lead to one of three scenarios: a change into something better, which does not exist and is impossible; a change into something worse, which is equally impossible and would imply God's corruption; or a change into something equally good, which also does not exist.

5. Scriptural Affirmations: Scripture not only declares God's general immutability (Malachi 3:6; James 1:17) but also underscores the immutability of His decrees (Isaiah 46:10; Psalms 33:12; Hebrews 6:17), emphasizing their steadfastness.

Objection

The only objection raised is based on certain passages of Scripture, which argue that promises and threats are conditioned. However, it is crucial to differentiate between promises and threats, which, although conditioned, are not properly described as mutable, and the decrees themselves. Any remaining controversies regarding this matter will be addressed, God willing, in their respective contexts within discussions on predestination, election, and reprobation.

The Practical Aspect

Now, as we transition to the practical dimension, we find that the divine decree, particularly in the context of predestination, election, and reprobation, holds profound significance. It is within this framework that we begin to unravel the majestic and perfect nature of God's lordship and sovereignty, attributes that have been ascribed to Him as marvelous and great in counsel (Isaiah 28:29; Jeremiah 32:19).

1. Extensive Sovereignty: The breadth of God's decree is awe-inspiring, encompassing every facet of the future. He orchestrates all things according to the counsel of His will (Ephesians 1:11; Psalms 115:3; Isaiah 46:10), ensuring that nothing occurs without His prior decree (Lamentations 3:37).

2. Independent Dominion: The governance of the world stands entirely on the predetermined sentence of the divine decree, free from dependency on any external factor (Romans 11:34–36).

3. Authoritative Omnipotence: God's decree bears the mark of His authority and omnipotence. His counsel remains steadfast, and He accomplishes all that He wills (Isaiah 46:10), rendering resistance to His will futile.

4. Divine Wisdom: Wisdom finds its home in God's counsel and statutes (Romans 11:33–34). It is in His counsel that wisdom

is preserved and celebrated, and His hypostatic Wisdom claims it as His own (Proverbs 8:14).

5. Unchanging Foundation: The divine decree is marked by constancy and immutability. It serves as the unshakable foundation of His dominion (2 Timothy 2:19).

6. Sovereign Liberty: God exercises His liberty in the free dispensation of all things from the counsel of His will alone, without any compulsion. He acts according to His own will, and His freedom shines brilliantly.

All these aspects combine to exalt the majesty of divine sovereignty. They call us to:

1. Acknowledge it (Psalms 93:1–2; 100:3).

2. Magnify and extol it (Psalms 99:1–5).

3. Humbly submit and bow before Him (Psalms 95:6).

4. Serve His counsel (Acts 13:36; Psalms 100:2).

5. Guarding Against Misuse of the Divine Decree

Secondly, in the realm of this subject, we must be vigilant against any misapplications of the divine decree. These include: (1) the imprudent probing of God's secret decree, a realm we are not meant to explore (Deuteronomy 29:29; Acts 1:7); (2) the disregard and contempt of God's decrees, treating them lightly (Isaiah 5:19; 2 Peter 3:4), and resisting them (Luke 7:30); (3) questioning the most wise and absolute decree of God, demanding reasons for it, as if our limited understanding could fathom His divine counsel (Job 38:2; Romans 9:20–21); (4) succumbing to indolence and neglecting the use of means, assuming that God, by an irrational decree, intends the end without requiring our active participation; or (5) falling into despair during hardships, falsely believing that we can discern God's secret counsel concerning our circumstances, or presuming to advise Him (Romans 11:34).

1. Embracing the Benefits of the Divine Decree

Conversely, thirdly, we must employ the contemplation of the divine decree for our own benefit. This includes: (1) fostering reverence for God, prompting repentance, and fleeing from sin, before the decree ushers in the day of judgment when we may perish like chaff (Zephaniah 2:2) or before it pronounces sudden destruction upon us (Jeremiah 18:7; Luke 19:42–43); (2) cultivating patience and inner peace in the face of adversities, recognizing that nothing, no matter how powerful, can befall us apart from what God's hand and counsel have ordained (Acts 4:27–28; 2:23), and trusting that everything, by the wisdom of His decree, ultimately works for our good (Romans 8:28); (3) finding confidence and peace in our salvation, as our redemption, justification, adoption, sanctification, and glorification rest upon God's eternal, wise, and unchanging decree, serving as a solid foundation and bearing the seal, "The Lord knows those who are His" (2 Timothy 2:19; Romans 8:29–30).

1. Emulating God's Wise Counsel in Worship

Lastly, we are called to emulate God's wisdom, especially in matters of divine worship. Just as God works with deliberate purpose and wise counsel, setting His glory as the ultimate goal, directing all things toward that purpose, and pursuing His design with unwavering determination, we too should follow this example. Since we are made in the image of God and our greatest perfection hinges upon imitating Him, it is imperative that in all aspects of our lives, especially in matters concerning God and our salvation, we act not on impulse or thoughtlessly but with careful deliberation, guided by divine decree and wise counsel (Ephesians 5:15). In doing so, our worship becomes reasonable and pleasing to God

(Romans 12:1). We ought to establish righteous goals—God's glory, our salvation, and the benefit of our neighbor—deliberately seek out the most effective means to achieve them, and pursue these goals with resolute determination.

Divine Predestination

"To demonstrate His wrath and make His power known, God endured with much patience the vessels of wrath prepared for destruction. In this way, He has revealed the riches of His glory to the vessels of mercy, whom He prepared in advance for glory." —Romans 9:22–23

Reflecting Upon Divine Predestination

I. The divine decree encompasses all creatures in one of two ways: either it pertains to all creatures without distinction regarding their every state, as seen in the decrees of creation (where creatures first come into existence) and providence (which governs their ongoing existence and directs them toward their ends); or it specifically concerns rational creatures. In the latter case, it addresses their temporal state, including the decree governing the end of their earthly lives, as well as their eternal state. This latter decree is commonly referred to as predestination. Our examination of predestination is grounded in the words of the apostle found in Romans 9:22–23.

The Exegetical Aspect

Drawing from Scriptural Exegesis

II. In these verses, the apostle elucidates the divine counsel of predestination concerning both its facets:

A. Regarding Reprobation (v. 22), which encompasses the following key elements:1. The Causal Agent of Reprobation, which also serves as the Agent of Election and consequently the common source for the entirety of predestination: "God." Here, "God" is understood as the initial and entirely independent cause, excluding any external motivating cause or condition that might influence God's decision in predestination. This term also excludes any intrinsic cause other than God's pure and unadulterated good pleasure or will, as signified by the term "willing" (θέλων). When used concerning creatures, "θέλων" sometimes conveys a desire or wish, albeit an ineffective one. This usage can be found both in secular authors (e.g., Cicero, Epistles to Familiars, bk. 15, epist. 7, "I will that the gods would bless you with that office") and sacred authors (e.g., Mark 10:35–36; Rom. 9:16). However, in the context of God and Christ, it denotes a purposeful intent (e.g., Matt. 8:3; Mark 1:41; Luke 5:13; John 3:8; 5:21; 21:22; Ps. 115:3; Eph. 1:5). Thus, it signifies that God's will or good pleasure is the sole and exclusive cause of the entire predestination process (Matt. 11:25–26), free from any dependence on anyone's choice (Rom. 9:16).2. The Objectives or Purposes of Reprobation, specifically aimed at revealing:a. Wrath: "to demonstrate his wrath" (ἐνδείξασθαι τὴν ὀργήν). Ὀργή, derived from ὀρέγεσθαι, meaning "to desire," refers to a desire for vengeance resulting from an inflicted injury. It is occasionally coupled with θυμός, signifying "burning anger" (Rom. 2:8). Wrath encompasses both a disturbance of the mind and a desire for vengeance: the former is conveyed by "θυμός," and the latter by "ὀργή." In God, there is no disturbance but only a desire for vengeance, akin to the avenging justice of God (John 3:36; Rom. 1:18). The term "ἐνδείξασθαι" emphasizes a clear and evident display (1 Tim. 1:16). This composite verb is used to describe both God (Rom. 9:17; Eph. 2:7) and humans (2 Cor. 8:24; 2 Tim. 4:14; Titus 2:10–11; 3:2), signifying a clear and unmistakable declaration that leaves no room for denial or concealment. The ultimate goal of reprobation is to manifest God's avenging justice through just punishment of the sinner, not the creature's destruction.b. Power: "and to make his power known" (γνωρίσαι τὸ δυνατὸν αὐτοῦ). Reprobation aims to reveal that God possesses the power to choose whomever He wills for the exercise of His avenging justice. This power is demonstrated through the act of reprobation, illustrating God's capability to select individuals from among all humanity. It is evident that the purpose of reprobation, like that of election, and thus the entire predestination process, is not merely to manifest God's common glory, a goal present in all of God's works. Instead, it primarily serves to manifest His unique glory, specifically in avenging justice, power, and mercy, showcased through righteous destruction and gracious salvation.c. Longsuffering within Reprobation, wherein God patiently "bore with much restraint of wrath" toward the reprobate. This means that despite their sins, God chose not to immediately destroy or withhold all kindness from them. Instead, His wrath was, so to speak, held in check, and they were showered with numerous blessings, both in the physical and spiritual realms. In this context, we witness not just one form of longsuffering but "manifold longsuffering" (πολλὴ μακροθυμία), as God is described as " ,□□□□ □□□slow to anger" (Joel 2:13). A person who is "μακρόθυμος," longsuffering, is far removed from "θυμός," or "burning anger." Some might translate this term as "magnanimity," signifying greatness of soul. This translation doesn't stem from the word's etymology or its inherent meaning, as "θυμός" doesn't refer to the soul but to "burning anger" or "wrath." However, it is appropriate to describe longsuffering as "magnanimity" in light of its results. A magnanimous individual can patiently endure numerous injuries inflicted upon them over an extended period and in a harsh manner. Thus, it is not unreasonable to use the term "magnanimity" to describe this aspect of God's character. Consequently, the secondary purpose of reprobation is founded on God's patience, forbearance, and magnanimity, and this serves a significant reason.

1. The Object of Reprobation: "Vessels of wrath," or instruments of wrath, are those through whom, or in their just condemnation, God reveals His wrath or punishing justice. The term "vessels" or "instruments" signifies any kind of apparatus, instrument, or utensils (Heb. 9:21). In this context, it refers to people, specifically the reprobate (2 Tim. 2:20–21). Through them or their rightful punishment, God typically manifests and upholds the glory of His avenging justice, power, and longsuffering. Conversely, the elect are referred to as "chosen vessels" (Acts 9:15) and "vessels for honor" (2 Tim. 2:21). They bring honor to God through their conversion and subsequent salvation, which highlights His grace and mercy.

2. The Act of Reprobation: "Prepared beforehand," indicating an eternal destination, "for destruction." This does not imply that God delights in the death of sinners (Ezek. 18:32). Instead, it signifies that they are "fitted," "joined," "adapted," or "made fit" for destruction. This participle serves as a verb, following Hebrew linguistic conventions, which tend to have fewer verbs. It's akin to the Hebrew (□□□□Ps. 68:10; 74:16), meaning "fit." It's often translated as ἑτοῖμος, "prepared," and sometimes as κατηρτισμένος. In Luke 6:40, it's taken similarly, implying "fit for destruction" in our text. But who fits them for destruction? They are partly responsible for this themselves through unbelief, impenitence, and their sinful choices, making themselves deserving of eternal destruction (Jude 4). Additionally, God plays a significant role, as He, through eternal reprobation, decreed to devote the impenitent to destruction (Prov. 16:4;

Matt. 25:34, 41). This is analogous to vessels being shaped by a potter (Jer. 18:6). The phrase "to destruction" carries a severe meaning. At its mildest, it signifies death (John 11:50), sometimes through wretched means like famine (Luke 15:17), and even eternal destruction (2 Thess. 1:9). Judas is called the "son of perdition" (John 17:12), and the devil is referred to as Ἀπολλύων, Apollyon, "the Destroyer" (Rev. 9:11). Hence, this phrase implies that through reprobation, the reprobate are prepared for various forms of destruction, both physical and spiritual, affecting both body and soul.

B. According to Election (v. 23), with its efficient cause presupposed:

1. Its Supreme End: "And that He might make known the riches of His glory." In this context, "glory" specifically refers to the goodness and mercy of God, as found in Exodus 33:18–19. The conjunction "and" (□or καὶ) links the preceding verse 22 with verse 23. This connection can be seen in two ways: first, by antithesis, it implies that the purpose of reprobation, albeit indirectly, is to showcase divine grace toward the vessels of mercy, which wouldn't be as apparent or valued if it were common to all. Second, it helps Paul to connect the other part of predestination, namely election, with the preceding reprobation. "Riches of His glory" (πλοῦτος τῆς δόξης) signifies the abundant and overflowing goodness and mercy of God, the riches of blessed immortality prepared in grace for the elect, or the richness of His glorious grace (Eph. 1:6, 14). Paul frequently uses "πλοῦτος" to refer to abundance (Rom. 2:4; 11:33; 2 Cor. 8:2; Eph. 1:7). Therefore, "πλοῦτος δόξης" here (and in Eph. 1:18; Col. 1:27) conveys an immense amount of glory.

2. Its Object: "Vessels of mercy" (σκεύη ἐλέους), in whom He would demonstrate the glory of His mercy through their gra-

cious restoration. "Ἔλεος" (mercy) carries the meaning of God's grace towards the suffering. It denotes all kinds of good things freely bestowed by God on humanity. When referring to God, it signifies His compassion and boundless kindness. Therefore, the elect are called "vessels of mercy" because they were chosen through divine mercy for the purpose of receiving mercy, and God intends to display the glory of His mercy through them.

3. The Act of Election: "Which He prepared beforehand for glory." God prepared them and made them fit for attaining salvation even before they existed, through His prior decree. This preparation does not assume any inherent aptitude but rather imparts and bestows it. "Ἑτοιμάζειν" (to prepare) signifies divine determination (Matt. 25:34; 1 Cor. 2:9; Heb. 11:16). "Προετοιμάζειν" means "to prepare beforehand," indicating that the act of election occurs long before good works and the calling to them. "Εἰς δόξαν" (for glory) refers not only to God's glory but also to the glory of the elect (2 Cor. 4:17).

The Dogmatic Part

The Existence of Predestination: Established by Scripture

III. Leaving aside the specific points in the text related to election and reprobation, it is undoubtedly clear that there exists a divine decree concerning the eternal destiny of rational creatures, which we refer to as predestination. This truth shines brighter than the sun, primarily through the testimony of Scripture. Scripture uses terms such as προορισμός (predestination, Rom. 8:29–30), πρόγνωσις (foreknowledge, Acts 2:23; 1 Peter 1:2; Rom. 8:29), πρόθεσις (purpose, Rom. 8:28; Eph. 1:9), and εὐδοκία (the good pleasure of the will, Matt. 11:26) when describing God's involvement in eternal salvation. It emphasizes that God acts solely according to the counsel of His will (Eph. 1:11) in matters of eternal salvation. Those destined for eternal salvation are described as τεταγμένοι εἰς ζωὴν αἰώνιον (appointed to eternal life, Acts 13:48), and they are also said to be προετοιμαζόμενοι εἰς δόξαν (prepared beforehand for glory, Rom. 9:23). Conversely, those facing damnation are described as κατηρτισμένοι εἰς ἀπώλειαν (fitted for destruction, Rom. 9:22) and προγεγραμμένοι εἰς τὸ κρίμα (marked out beforehand for condemnation, Jude 4).

Reasons Supporting Predestination

IV. The existence of predestination is evident not only from Scripture but also from nature. (1) Since God governs all things according to the counsel of His will, even the smallest matters, would He then neglect such a crucial matter as the eternal destiny of rational creatures? (2) Without an eternal decree, no aspect of the future could exist unless God were subject to change over time or dependent on something else. In such a case, everything would be subject to an unavoidable fate, which is contrary to God's sovereignty. It follows that neither the salvation nor the destruction of a creature can occur without eternal predestination. (3) The glory of God arising from the eternal salvation or destruction of creatures would be greatly diminished if it were established that these events happen by chance, without the prior eternal counsel of God. (4) Furthermore, the fullness of divine glory is manifest when predestination includes both vessels of wrath and vessels of grace within God's house (2 Tim. 2:20).

Clarity in Terminology

V. We have already discussed the various synonyms for predestination, but it is beneficial to emphasize that προορισμός, predestination, sometimes has a broader meaning, encompassing any divine decree (Acts 4:28; 1 Cor. 2:7). On the other hand, πρόγνωσις, foreknowledge, refers to God's prior knowledge and predilection, which forms the basis for election (Rom. 8:29). Alternatively, it may denote the comprehensive concept of God's entire predestining counsel in His divine mind, existing prior to the creation of all things. Additionally, πρόθεσις, purpose, at times specifically pertains to the aspect of predestination that intends the end or outlines the means to reach that end. In this stricter sense, it is termed predestination. Thus, predestination is occasionally said to occur according to God's purpose, and His purpose aligns with election, which is itself according to God's purpose, counsel, and good pleasure (Eph. 1:5).

Understanding the Term Predestination

VI. The term predestination can be used interchangeably with election in certain contexts (Rom. 8:29). However, within the realm of election itself, it can more strictly refer to God's predetermined arrangement of means leading to the salvation of the elect, following His foreknowledge: "Those whom he foreknew, he predestined." In this discussion, we use the term predestination broadly, encompassing the entirety of God's plan concerning the eternal state of rational creatures. It is termed "destination" because it signifies the determination of the order of means leading to their ends. It is called "predestination" because God established this order for Himself before the existence of all things.

The Essence of Predestination

VII. In essence, predestination is nothing other than God's divine decree concerning the manifestation of His unique glory in the eternal state of rational creatures. It is referred to as a decree because it comprises a definitive pronouncement by God, executed according to His certain counsel. Consequently, what was previously discussed in the preceding chapter regarding God's general decree finds application here to elucidate the concept of predestination.

Significance of Predestination: Three Aspects

VIII. Within predestination, there exist three significant aspects. Firstly, it encompasses the proposed end, which is the declaration of God's glory. However, it is not just any form of glory but specifically, (1) the glory of His divine authority and dominion, as indicated in Romans 9:22, "willing to make his power known," and in verse 21, "Does not the potter have authority over the clay?" This reflects His ability to designate His creatures, regardless of their freedom, for purposes aligned with His pure, unadulterated good pleasure, assigning one as a vessel of wrath and another as a vessel of glory. (2) The glory of His grace and mercy, as seen in "to the praise of his glorious grace" (Eph. 1:6), is evident in His decree to restore creatures deserving only wrath and eternal condemnation, not only to eternal life but also through the death of His own and only begotten Son. (3) The glory of His avenging justice, as highlighted in "willing to show his wrath" (Rom. 9:22), pertains to the just condemnation of rebellious creatures.

Selection of Means and Its Conception

IX. Secondly, predestination encompasses the idea and conception of the means, as well as the discernment involved in selecting the most appropriate means. These means encompass: (1) Gratuitous salvation and just condemnation, representing the decision to manifest the glory of His grace and justice through them. (2) The entire creation of the human race, along with the establishment and abandonment of the covenant of works or the permission of the fall. This was done so that there would be an object in which He could manifest the glory of His mercy and wrath, all of which amalgamate as one means within the scope of predestination. (3) The selection of individual persons from the entirety of created beings, specifically chosen to reveal His mercy and wrath in a profound manner.

Purpose of Predestination: Three Aspects

X. Thirdly, within predestination lies the purpose and destination of the means through which God would bring about the free salvation of some and the just condemnation of others. This involves the restoration of the former through the Son, acting as the Mediator, and the abandonment of the latter in their sins. More will be expounded on these matters in their respective contexts.

Predestination: A Fusion of Intellect and Will

XI. Consequently, predestination is not solely an act of the intellect or will, as asserted by some Scholastics, but rather a harmonious combination of both intellect and will. It is referred to as counsel, wherein the concept formed by the mind regarding the end and means aligns with the intention of the will. It is also referred to as foreknowledge, preordained plan, and the counsel of His will. This applies not only to election but also to reprobation. Therefore, as the apostle declares, "willing to show his wrath," this applies to every divine decree, as God orchestrates all things according to the counsel of His will (Eph. 1:11).

Focus on Rational Creatures: Angels

XII. Predestination, distinct from the general decree, primarily pertains to rational creatures—both angels and humans. Every one of them is encompassed within its scope because they are subject to the eternal state, within which the unique glory of God can and should be revealed through salvation and condemnation. Scripture affirms the angels as objects of predestination, explicitly mentioning the elect angels (1 Tim. 5:21; Matt. 25:34, 41) and those reserved for judgment in chains of darkness (2 Peter 2:4; Jude 6; Matt. 25:41, 34).

Regarding Humanity

However, the Scriptures provide more abundant insight into the predestination of humanity. Both angels and humans, as rational creatures, are the subjects of predestination concerning their eternal state—either destruction or glory (Rom. 9:22–23). In terms of their temporal state, they are subject to the common decree of providence, just like all other creatures. Moreover, both angels and humans are objects of predestination, not in their created and fallen state. It's evident that angels cannot be considered in predestination as created and fallen. To illustrate this more clearly in the context of humans, we must examine these four acts of God: (1) His purpose to manifest the glory of His mercy and avenging justice; (2) His decision to create all humans and permit them to fall through a common ancestor; (3) His determination to elect certain individuals from the created and fallen humanity, thereby manifesting the glory of His mercy, and to reprobate others, manifesting the glory of His avenging justice; (4) His intention to prepare and direct the means corresponding to election and reprobation. In the first act of predestination, the object could only be humanity, capable of being created and falling, as no decree has yet been made concerning creation and the fall. In the second act, the object is humanity, to be created and to fall. In the third act, the object is humanity, created and fallen. In the fourth act, the object is humanity, elected and reprobated. Therefore, since predestination, when distinguished from election and reprobation, encompasses the two prior acts, it is most accurate to say that the object of predestination is humanity, capable of being created and capable of falling, followed by humanity, to be created and to fall. Conversely, the objects of election and reprobation are humanity, created and fallen. This reconciles differing opinions and resolves the disputes that often arise. When supralapsarians confront infralapsarians with Scripture passages where God predestines humanity as vessels of wrath and mercy, the infralapsarians can respond by emphasizing that the object of predestination, particularly its first act or purpose, is humanity, created and fallen. This clarifies the issue and eliminates misunderstandings. Conversely, if supralapsarians argue that infralapsarians propose a creation and fall without the purpose of manifesting grace and justice, it can be countered that the purpose of creation and the permitted fall is, indeed, to manifest grace and justice, with the object being humanity, capable of being created and capable of falling. However, the object of election and reprobation, in and of itself, is humanity, created and fallen.

Various Opinions on the Object of Predestination

It is worthwhile to explore the differences in opinions on this matter. The rigid supralapsarians argue that individuals like Peter and Judas are the object of predestination only in the sense that they are still capable of being created and capable of falling. Conversely, the rigid infralapsarians maintain that the object of predestination is solely humanity created and fallen. The theologians who hold a middle and orthodox position assert that the object of predestination, as such, is humanity capable of being created and capable of falling, while the object of election and reprobation, as such, is humanity created and fallen. Reformed universalists contend that the object of election and reprobation includes humanity that is also redeemed and called, while Pelagians and those influenced by Pelagianism argue that it encompasses both believing and unbelieving individuals, even at the moment of death and in a state of spiritual death.

The Properties of Predestination

When considering the properties of predestination, as with any of God's divine decrees, we find that it is first and foremost eternal (Rom. 9:11; Eph. 1:4; 2 Tim. 1:9; 2 Thess. 2:13). It has been at work from the very beginning of God's works, yet it does not affect any differences among the predestined until their actual calling (Eph. 2:3). Predestination, before the application of grace, which takes place in effectual calling or, more precisely, in regeneration, does not introduce any change in the predestined individuals but remains concealed solely within the One who predestines.

Furthermore, secondly, predestination is independent because it serves as the primary determining cause of the eternal state. God is "willing to show his wrath" and more (Rom. 9:22–23). Therefore: (1) Predestination does not necessarily require either its object or its outcome to already exist but establishes its object in a way that ensures its existence, such that by the power of predestination, it is ordained to come into being (1 Peter 1:20). (2) It does not rely on any external cause, reason, or condition but proceeds solely from the will of the One who predestines (Matt. 11:26; Rom. 9:16, 18). Thus, (3) it is neither logical nor consistent with the Scriptures to posit any prerequisite quality in humanity as if it were the formal object of predestination or to attribute any particular state to humanity in such a manner that others are excluded. It is enough to recognize that all people are the object of this distinct decree, making them equal among themselves. The differences among individuals result from this decree, and these distinctions are not contingent upon humanity but are revealed through it.

1. Unchangeability

Moving on, thirdly, predestination is characterized by its unchangeability, a quality shared with other divine decrees (Isa. 14:26–27; 46:10). It is often referred to as the firm foundation of God (2 Tim. 2:19), marked by an unbreakable seal. Once someone is elected, they will never be reprobated, and conversely, once someone is reprobated, they will never be elected.

1. Certainty

Fourthly, predestination brings certainty, precisely determining the number of those who will be saved and those who will be condemned. It not only calculates the abstract quantity of those to be saved or damned but also specifies the concrete individuals who will be part of these groups (2 Tim. 2:19). Predestination doesn't merely decide the general destiny of the saved and the damned ("I will save believers, I will condemn unbelievers"), but it also designates the particular persons ("He has mercy on whom he wills, and he hardens whom he wills," Rom. 9:18), even down to the individual level ("Jacob I have loved, Esau I have hated," Rom. 9:13).

1. Absoluteness

Fifthly, predestination is absolute and definitive. While it links salvation and condemnation to their respective causes and conditions, and can therefore be considered conditioned to some extent, it remains itself unconditionally grounded. Those whom God foreknew, He predestined; those whom He predestined, He called; those whom He called, He justified; and finally, those whom He justified, He also glorified (Rom. 8:29–30).

1. Freedom

Sixthly, predestination operates with a remarkable freedom. God exercises His mercy and hardening as He wills, shaping vessels for honor and dishonor like a potter forming vessels from the same lump according to His sovereign pleasure (Rom. 9:18, 21). His choices are not constrained by natural necessity or determined by the condition of the object but are solely guided by the pure and unadulterated good pleasure of His will (Matt. 11:25–26).

1. Divine Wisdom

Seventh, and finally, predestination is marked by divine wisdom. It is aptly described by the apostle who exclaimed, "Oh, the depth of the riches of the wisdom and knowledge of God! How unsearchable are his judgments, and his paths beyond tracing out!" (Rom. 11:33–34). Indeed, God's wisdom in predestination is profound and beyond human comprehension. It is often referred to as counsel because it reflects the supreme wisdom that God employs in His deliberate plans. While God is not reliant on external causes or reasons, He always possesses His own rationale for His divine counsel. He intricately weaves the means with the ends He desires to achieve, carefully selecting the means that align with His purposes.

The Divine Order in Predestination

Twenty-firstly, the profound order of predestination is a recurring theme in Scripture (Rom. 8:28–30; 9:11; Eph. 1:4–5; 1 Thess. 5:9; 2 Thess. 2:13–14; 1 Peter 1:2; John 3:16). It is marked by divine wisdom, evident through the deliberate subordination and arrangement of ends and means, causes and effects. This order is vividly displayed in the execution of salvation and condemnation. A guiding principle for this order is captured in the adage, "Whatever is first in intention is last in execution," and conversely, "Whatever is last in execution was first in intention." In accordance with this principle, God purposed: (1) to reveal the glory of His grace and justice; (2) to create humanity in His image, entering into a covenant of works and permitting the fall; (3) to individually elect some and reject others from the fallen human race; (4) to provide the means of salvation to the elect, including redemption through the Mediator, Jesus Christ, and the application of redemption through faith, while denying these means to the reprobate; (5) to save the elect eternally through faith in Christ and condemn the reprobate eternally for their sins; and ultimately, (6) to glorify His mercy in the salvation of the elect and His avenging justice in the condemnation of the reprobate. Scripture upholds this order, and experience bears witness to its truth.

Predestination of Angels and Humans

Twenty-secondly, predestination pertains to either angels or humans, as previously mentioned. Regarding the predestination of angels, Scripture provides limited explicit information, with additional insights gleaned from the execution of God's divine decree and through comparison with the predestination of humans.

Similarities between the predestination of angels and humans include: (1) the divine good pleasure as the efficient and compelling cause, for God chose angels (1 Tim. 5:21; cf. Mark 13:20) and reprobated those for whom He prepared eternal fire (Matt. 25:41), all according to His sovereign will (Dan. 4:25); (2) the formal act of predestination, involving the separation or discrimination of angels to be preserved or abandoned, as implied in election (1 Tim. 5:21) and illustrated by God's judgment upon the angels who sinned (2 Peter 2:4); (3) the ultimate purpose of predestination, which is to reveal grace, at least preserving grace, and punitive justice; (4) the object of predestination being capable of creation, capable of falling, created, and fallen.

Distinguishing Differences

However, distinctions exist between them: (1) in chronological order, with the predestination of angels preceding that of humans, as indicated in Matthew 25:41 and reflected in the sequence of their creation; (2) in their primary cause, with grace being the basis for the preservation of angels and mercy for the restoration of humanity; (3) in means and outcomes, as God does not employ Christ the Mediator or the processes of calling, justification, and adoption in the beatification of angels, unlike in the case of humans; (4) in intensity, where the election of angels reflects greater grace, preserving them from misery, and their reprobation reflects a greater rigor of justice, casting them away without hope of restoration (2 Peter 2:4). In contrast, the election of humanity reveals greater mercy as God saves sinful humans, but it also demonstrates greater severity as the reprobate are held accountable not only for their actual sins but also for original sin and the transgression of their first parents.

The Components of Predestination: Election and Reprobation

Twenty-thirdly, predestination, whether concerning angels or humans, consists of two essential components: election and reprobation. While Scripture emphasizes election more prominently in the context of predestination, the rationale for this distinction will be explored in the forthcoming sections, with individual attention given to each component in their respective chapters.

The Elenctic Section

1. Is Reprobation a Component of Predestination?

Twenty-fourthly, we must inquire whether reprobation constitutes a part or category of predestination. This inquiry could involve the terminology itself, pondering whether the term "predestination" also encompasses reprobation. Alternatively, it could explore the substantial question of whether God has a decree concerning the eternal state of the reprobate, akin to the decree regarding the eternal state of the elect.

A Survey of Different Views

Among the papists and Scholastics, who strive to maintain the independence and indifference of free will, asserting that this is necessitated by divine decree, they deny any divine decree in reprobation. Instead, they acknowledge only mere foreknowledge, as this foreknowledge does not influence or impose necessity upon the free choices of the reprobate. They liken it to a physician's foreknowledge of a patient's death, which does not compel the patient's demise. Consequently, they refuse to equate reprobation with predestination. On the other hand, Lutherans, motivated by their aversion to the absolute decree in reprobation, limit the discussion of predestination to election alone.

The Position of the Reformed and Their Rationale

In contrast, the Reformed perspective maintains that God has decreed the eternal state of the reprobate as much as He has for the elect. Thus, reprobation is viewed as a form of predestination, although they do not engage in disputes over terminology. Their arguments are chiefly based on the following considerations:

1. The term "predestination" is closely associated with reprobation, as evidenced by its usage in Acts 4:28 (and in connection to the reprobate Judas in Acts 1:16 and 1:25).

2. Scripture attributes the substance of predestination to reprobation in several instances. Proverbs 16:4 suggests that God made the wicked for the day of evil, and Matthew 25:41 states that eternal fire was prepared for the devil, his angels, and the reprobate before the foundations of the world. Romans 9:22 speaks of vessels of wrath prepared beforehand for destruction, and 1 Thessalonians 5:9 mentions some being appointed for wrath, with Jude 4 discussing those marked out for condemnation.

3. In Romans 9:17-18, Pharaoh's blindness and hardness, which are means of reprobation, are attributed to the predestinating

will of God. Unbelievers destined for stumbling are mentioned in 1 Peter 2:8.

4. Reprobation involves the allocation of means to an end, similar to election. Just as the vessels of mercy are destined for the manifestation of God's glorious grace, the vessels of wrath or the reprobate are destined for the manifestation of His wrath or avenging justice (Romans 9:22-23).

5. Early church figures such as Augustine (in his Enchiridion and On the Merits and Forgiveness of Sins), Prosper of Aquitaine (in his Responses to the Propositions of the Gauls), and Fulgentius of Ruspe (in his treatise On Double Predestination) concur with this viewpoint, asserting that reprobation is indeed a form of predestination, aligning with both Scripture and the Reformed perspective.

Objections Addressed

However, objections are raised against this view:

1. They argue that the term "predestination" (προορισμός) is not found in the Scriptures concerning reprobation. In response, (a) it is acknowledged that this term does not explicitly apply to reprobation in Scripture. Nevertheless, we do not engage in semantic disputes as long as the substance of the doctrine remains intact. (b) The term and its related forms are used in Scripture regarding reprobation, as previously demonstrated.

2. Another objection is based on Romans 8:29-30, which states that those who have been predestined are also glorified, yet the reprobate are not glorified. Therefore, they argue that the reprobate cannot be predestined. In response, (a) this objection would also imply that the reprobate are not foreknown, which contradicts opposing views. (b) While Romans 8:28 uses the

term "predestination" more strictly in the context of election, it is employed in a related form concerning reprobation in Acts 4:28.

3. It is argued that in reprobation, there is no foreordination of the end and means, as neither damnation (considered evil) nor sin (a means of reprobation) can be destined to an end. In response, the end of reprobation is not damnation itself, but rather the manifestation of God's avenging justice and power (Romans 9:22). The means are the just condemnation imposed due to the sins of the reprobate. God has harmoniously connected these means to the intended end in reprobation, making it an act of divine destination.

4. Another objection asserts that election and reprobation are opposed, and therefore, they cannot fall under the same category of predestination. In response, (a) just as man and beast, despite their differences, share a common proximate genus, so do election and reprobation, albeit different, belong to the same genus of predestination (1 Thessalonians 5:9). (b) While their objects and effects are opposing, they are not opposed with respect to God, but rather differ. Both originate from the one predestinating God and His sovereign good pleasure (Matthew 11:25-26).

5. It is contended that if reprobation were considered a form of predestination, then the reprobate would be predestined to sin and eternal damnation. In response, this is not the case. The reprobate is predestined to serve as a display of God's avenging justice and power as the ultimate end, along with just condemnation due to their sins as the means.

6. Lastly, it is argued that if reprobation were a type of predes-

tination, then the reprobate would not sin freely and would not be justly condemned. In response, despite predestination, the reprobate still sins freely, making choices based on counsel, deliberation, and rational decision. Predestination does not impede this freedom. After freely sinning, they are justly condemned as a result.

The Singular Nature of Predestination

Now we must contemplate whether predestination, especially eternal and absolute predestination, can be condensed into a singular concept: that God decreed from eternity to elect the compliant and to condemn the noncompliant. Our opponents, the Socinians and Arminians, propose various forms of divine predestination, some eternal and some temporal. Among the eternal predestinations, they distinguish two: one absolute, concerning the state, in which God decrees to save the compliant and condemn the noncompliant; the other conditional, concerning persons, like, "I will to save Peter if he chooses to render himself compliant, and to condemn Judas if he chooses not to render himself compliant." They also posit a temporal predestination, which can be further divided into non-peremptory, such as "I will to save eternally Peter, whom I presently see believes, if he continues in faith to the end," and peremptory, like "Because I see that at the moment of death he chooses to endure, I will to save him eternally." Conversely, they say, "I will to damn Judas eternally because I see he chooses not to believe." Their fundamental error lies in preserving the notion of independent indifference in human free choice, which they believe is compromised or obliterated by an eternal, absolute, and personal decree.

The Perspective of the Reformed with Supporting Arguments

The Reformed perspective, in contrast, affirms only one predestination: it is eternal, absolute, and personal. The key reasons for this position include:

1. Because every divine decree is a manifestation of God Himself, as discussed in the previous chapter.

2. All divine decrees are eternal in nature, consistent with the previous chapter's findings.

3. There is no room for conditioned decrees of God, as outlined in the same chapter.

4. General decrees of God are not recognized, as explained in the same chapter.

5. Mutable decrees of God are not accepted, as detailed in the same chapter.

6. Scripture directly applies predestination to individual persons, such as Jacob and Esau (Romans 9:10-12), the apostles (Luke 10:20), and Paul (Acts 9:15), among others.

7. God's knowledge of His own is derived from predestination (2 Timothy 2:19).

8. Paul consistently extends the concept of predestination to himself and his audience, as seen in passages concerning the Ephesians, Thessalonians, and others (Ephesians 1:4-5; 2 Thessalonians 2:13; 1 Thessalonians 5:9).

9. Through predestination, specific individuals are effectively inscribed into the book of life (Revelation 13:8; Daniel 12:1; Luke 10:20; Philippians 4:3; Revelation 20:15; 21:26).

10. Paul emphasizes the connection between foreknowledge and predestination (Romans 8:29-30). Moreover, the Scriptures affirm that "as many as were appointed to eternal life believed"

(Acts 13:48). Our opponents, however, cannot produce any scriptural passage that explicitly denies individual predestination or limits it solely to determining the salvation or damnation of individuals.

Challenges and Responses

Now, let us address the objections raised against the concept of individual predestination:

1. Some argue that passages of Scripture speaking of promises and threats differ greatly from the idea of decree and predestination. As we previously demonstrated in the preceding chapter, these are indeed distinct concepts (§XXXII).

2. Concerns have been raised that predestination negates the contingency of events and the freedom of choice, pushing everything into the realm of hard necessity. This, however, is consistently denied. Predestination does not obstruct the occurrence of many events in the world through proximate causes that are not inherently predetermined, making them contingent. It also allows for events driven by causes that act by their own counsel, illustrating the concept of liberty. Instead, predestination simply determines the certainty of outcomes to be achieved, whether through necessary, contingent, or free causes, as we have discussed elsewhere.

3. It has been argued that individual predestination contradicts all forms of religion and divine worship because they are perceived as incompatible with necessity. This argument, however, loses its ground when the previous notion that predestination implies necessity has already been refuted.

4. Lastly, the objection is raised that individual predestination portrays God in an unworthy light, attributing to Him:

(a) Iniquity, as it appears that He punishes individuals for actions they were unable to avoid due to His decree. In response, God punishes not because someone acts in accordance with His decree, but because they willingly transgress the law given to them, unaware of His decree, and motivated by their own desires.

(b) Deceptive pretense, as it seems God calls all to salvation while, by an unchangeable decree, He knows that the majority will not be saved. In reply, God's call is not to ensure their salvation but rather to render them without excuse, allowing them to perish due to their own stubbornness.

(c) Ignorance and imprudence, as God earnestly calls and attempts to lead to salvation those whom He foreknows, through predestination, will never attain salvation. In return, His call and efforts are intended not for their actual salvation but for them to face the consequences of their voluntary obstinacy.

(d) Depravity, as it is suggested that God not only decreed who would be condemned but also who would sin. In rebuttal, God decreed to allow sin and, based on it, to justly condemn, so that His justice would be made manifest, devoid of any form of depravity.

The Divine Will in Predestination

Let us explore the question of whether, beyond the divine good pleasure, there exists any motivating cause for predestination:

1. Some hold extreme Pelagian views, shared by modern Socinians, which deny the existence of any certain foreknowledge of free future events. They argue that such knowledge cannot exist due to the independent indifference of free choice. In this view, foreseeing faith, repentance, or divine good pleasure is not considered the motivating cause of predestination.

2. Others, such as semi-Pelagians, papists, Remonstrants, Lutherans, and those outside the Reformed church, propose different motivating causes. They suggest that predestination is impelled

by foreseen good works for election (as asserted by papists), or foreseen faith for election and foreseen unbelief for reprobation (as claimed by others). These views aim to preserve the notion of independent human free will.

The Reformed perspective, however, does not attribute a specific cause to predestination. According to Reformed theology, predestination itself is God, the predestinating agent, who exists independently and is not subject to cause and effect relationships. While, from a human perspective, we may speak of God's good pleasure as the impelling cause of predestination, we distinguish reasons from causes. Reasons provide the basis for connecting means with ends, while causes produce effects. Thus, the reason behind God's good pleasure is understood to be the manifestation of His mercy and avenging justice. However, no cause or reason outside of God Himself is admitted for predestination except His own good pleasure. Here are our reasons:

1. The Scriptures do not reveal any external impelling cause or reason beyond God's good pleasure (Matthew 11:25–26; Ephesians 1:5; Romans 9:22–23, etc.).

2. In those who are predestined and will eventually exist in time, there can be nothing that might serve as a cause for eternal predestination. To assert otherwise would imply that something arising in time is the cause of what was eternally decreed.

3. All things in the predestined, which may be considered causes, follow predestination itself. This includes good works (Ephesians 1:4), faith (Acts 13:48), and unbelief (John 8:47; 6:65).

4. God's foreknowledge of who will believe and who will not is inseparable from the decree of predestination, as all future events stem from God's decree alone.

5. To suggest that individuals make themselves differ from one another contradicts the teaching of the Apostle Paul in 1 Corinthians 4:7: "Who makes you to differ? And what do you have that you did not receive? And if you did receive it, why do you boast as if you had not received it?"

Addressing Objections

Now, let us address some objections raised against the concept of predestination:

1. It is argued that Christ is the cause of divine good pleasure and, consequently, of predestination, especially electing predestination (Matthew 3:17; 17:5; Isaiah 42:1). In response, we acknowledge that in Christ, the Father finds pleasure in the context of the eternal counsel of peace. The Father appointed Christ as the Promisor of the elect, the exclusive Mediator for them, accepted His satisfaction for their guilt, and recognized Him as the meritorious source of all saving benefits according to election. However, when it comes to the act of predestination or election itself, signifying God's choosing, Christ is not referred to as its cause.

2. It is further argued that we cannot find favor with God to be elected through predestination unless we are in Christ (Ephesians 1:5). Moreover, we cannot be in Christ except through faith. Therefore, it is suggested that the cause of predestination includes not only the divine good pleasure but also Christ and foreseen faith in Him. In response, we affirm that it is indeed true that we cannot please God without Christ (Ephesians 1:5–7) or without faith (Hebrews 11:6). Nevertheless, this fact does not negate the pure, unadulterated good pleasure of God in predestining both Christ and faith for the elect. It is through Christ and faith that they find favor with God. The good plea-

sure of giving Christ and faith is rooted in God's sovereign will, and it is by His grace that they are destined to please Him through Christ and faith.

3. It is argued that if predestination is absolute, meaning it is independent of foreseen events, then glorification should also be absolute because it is said to result from divine good pleasure (Luke 12:32). However, this argument is deemed flawed because glorification is contingent upon calling and justification (Romans 8:29–30). In response, we clarify that there is no necessary connection between absolute predestination and absolute glorification. From the standpoint of absolute predestination and the divine good pleasure, glorification hinges on faith and holiness. While the consequence of predestination is tied to faith, the act of predestination itself, as seen in Romans 8:29–30, is not.

4. Finally, it is suggested that if predestination depends solely on divine good pleasure, an elect individual could live impiously to the end and still be saved, while a reprobate individual living piously could be damned. In response, we affirm that from the standpoint of predestination, an elect person cannot persist in living impiously until the end of their life (Ephesians 1:4). Conversely, a reprobate individual, predestined as such, cannot genuinely live piously. Predestination encompasses both the end and the appropriate means, ensuring that the elect are guided in faith and holiness.

Concerning the Arminian Order of Predestination

Now, let us examine the Arminian order of predestination, a perspective also adopted, with minor variations, by the Jesuits and Lutherans. In this order, God ordained the following sequence:

1. God determined to provide Christ as the Mediator to abolish sin through His sacrificial death.

2. God decided to extend His grace to those who repent and believe, while condemning those who remain impenitent and unbelieving.

3. God purposed to offer sufficient and effective means for repentance and faith to all.

4. Lastly, God chose by name those whom He foresaw would willingly believe, and He reprobated those whom He foresaw would not believe.

In response to this order, it must be emphasized that the foundation of this perspective rests on the following principles:

1. The belief in a universal grace equally available to all in the first three acts.

2. The concept of free will, which allows individuals to choose to believe or not believe, resulting in distinctions within the universal grace.

3. A predestination that depends on the creature's free choices.

4. A predestination primarily concerned with the state of individuals rather than the individuals themselves.

However, it should be firmly stated that this order fundamentally contradicts both the teachings of Scripture and real-life experiences. This contradiction is meticulously elucidated by Alting in his New Elenctic Theology (loc. 4, controv. 2). Further exploration of the nuances and divisions within predestination will be addressed specifically in the chapters on election and reprobation.

The Practical Aspect

Now, as we explore the realm of predestination, particularly within its specific aspects of election and reprobation, we must reflect on several crucial principles. These principles guide our understanding and application of God's divine plan.

First and foremost, we must acknowledge (1) the absolute sovereignty and authority of God. In this divine authority, we find that God possesses the power to direct not only the lower beings but also the most exalted, including angels and humans, determining their eternal destinies, be it salvation or condemnation. His authority encompasses not only their temporal states but also their eternal fates, and all of this is achieved according to His divine purpose and pleasure. The apostle passionately emphasizes this authority, as we see in Romans 9:17, "For this very purpose I have raised you up, that I may show my authority in you," and further expounds in verses 21 and 22.

Moreover, (2) God's independence is a critical aspect of predestination. He does not rely on the worthiness or unworthiness of any creature in His grand design but solely on His pure, unadulterated good pleasure. As we learn from Romans 9:11 and subsequent verses, God's choices are not determined by works, and He loves and hardens hearts according to His will.

Furthermore, (3) God's wisdom shines brightly in predestination. He knows how to employ the most effective means and opportune moments for His divine purposes. This wisdom is beyond our comprehension, as expressed by the apostle in Romans 11:33-34. It is imperative that we approach predestination with reverence rather than scrutiny, submit ourselves humbly to His will, and glorify Him, for "who will resist His will?" (Rom. 9:19).

Secondly, let us exercise great caution in the realm of predestination, for within this profound mystery lie potential dangers that could lead us astray if not approached with reverence and wisdom. These hazards include:

(1) The temptation to look too deeply into the reasons behind predestination, seeking to comprehend why God chose one path over another, or why He elected one and not another. This, in essence, amounts to demanding that the inscrutable ways of God conform to our limited understanding. It is akin to questioning the independent God about His divine counsel, which is a futile endeavor, as expressed in Romans 11:33. We must resist the presumption of thinking ourselves wiser than the Most Wise.

(2) The danger of disputing and criticizing the justice of predestination, implying that God shows favoritism or bestows unequal gifts upon equals. This challenges His sovereignty and authority, and it reduces us to the role of judges over the Supreme Judge, as seen in passages like Romans 9:14 and Matthew 20:11-14. We must remember that God owes nothing to anyone, especially to sinners, except for the judgment they deserve.

(3) The risk of misconstruing predestination as absolute necessity, thereby negating human free will and undermining the importance of religious diligence and the means of salvation. Predestination does not eliminate our freedom of choice; rather, it directs it toward God's ordained purposes. We should not fall into despair, echoing, "Who will resist His will?" (Romans 9:19).

(4) The peril of attributing sin to God as the author of sin. God's decrees do not cause future sins but only determine their occurrence in the divine plan, as explained in previous chapters.

(5) The potential for despair, assuming that we have a complete understanding of the inscrutable and unsearchable counsel of predestination, or worse, that we have acted as counselors to the predestinating God (Romans 8:33-34).

(6) Lastly, the temptation to succumb to apathy and negligence, dismissing the importance of care and the means of salvation because God's predestined counsel remains unchangeable. This is akin to assuming that the wise Creator has decreed the end without considering the means, or foolishly concluding that our actions are irrelevant to the divine plan. Such thinking is far from the truth, and we should uphold the significance of both God's sovereignty and human responsibility in the grand scheme of predestination.

Thirdly, let us contemplate the divine decree of predestination in a way that draws us to care diligently for our eternal state. When we consider that God, from all eternity, has taken such profound care for each individual and their eternal destiny that He ordained a specific decree for it, our hearts should be stirred. In this decree, God has destined every person and their entire eternal state for the sole purpose of manifesting His own glory. He created all individuals and all things with this ultimate goal in mind. Some were chosen for the glory of His grace, while others were rejected for the glory of His justice. God diligently applies the means of grace to the elect and the means of justice to the rejected, demonstrating His unfathomable wisdom. As we reflect on God's eternal care for us and our eternal state, it should ignite a deep sense of concern within us.

If God, from eternity past, had such profound care for us, how much more should we care for ourselves and our own eternal destiny? Let us exercise this care with unwavering determination, aligning our goals with God's glory. With Him as our guide, we should diligently pursue our eternal well-being through appropriate means. As we navigate life's challenges, let us remember that "we look not at the things which are seen, but at the things which are not seen, for the things which are seen are temporary, whereas the things which are not seen are eternal" (2 Corinthians 4:18).

May we approach this task with a wise and unshakable resolve, acknowledging that our ultimate aim is the glory of God. Let us earnestly work out our salvation with fear and trembling, knowing that it is God who works within us, both to will and to do according to His good pleasure (Philippians 2:12-13). Dr. Hoornbeeck's insights in his Practical Theology, particularly in Book 1, Chapter 1, and Book 2, Chapter 2, offer valuable guidance on the practical aspects of predestination. For a more detailed exploration of related topics, refer to the chapters on election and reprobation.

Election

"As He chose us in Him before the foundations of the world were laid, that we should be holy and blameless before Him in love, He who predestined us to adopt us as sons through Jesus Christ to Himself, according to the good pleasure of His will, to the praise of His glorious grace." — Ephesians 1:4–6

A Contemplation on Election

I. According to the dialecticians' doctrine, every species absorbs and encompasses the entire nature of its genus, as well as what is specific to its own species. Similarly, as predestination encompasses the complete nature of the divine decree, of which it is a species, election and reprobation, being species of predestination, contain all that is within both the decree and predestination. Recognizing this point, when carefully considered, allows for a concise presentation of both these species. With this perspective in mind, let us now descend from predestination to explore the concept of election. The Apostle Paul provides a detailed description of its nature in Ephesians 1:4-6.

The Exegetical Part

Rooted in Scriptural Interpretation

II. Within these words, we find a meticulous depiction of election, dissecting its parts or actions alongside all relevant details. There are, in essence, two primary actions:

A. Election in its strictest sense. While considering election more broadly, we discern four distinct actions: (1) the intent to reveal mercy; (2) the purpose behind creating those chosen, including their fall, to serve as vessels for the display of divine mercy; (3) the selection of specific individuals through whom God would manifest His mercy; and finally, (4) the predestination of the means by which the elect would attain this mercy. The initial two actions are more appropriately associated with predestination in a general sense, while the latter two actions specifically concern election. In our text, the apostle deliberately explores these two actions. First, he explores election, as evident in verse 4, "Even as He chose us in Him before the foundations of the world were laid, that we should be holy and blameless before Him in love." These words unveil:

1. The Act of Election: "just as he chose" (καθὼς ἐξελέξατο). The term καθὼς connects the previous verse (verse 3) with verse 4, emphasizing that all spiritual blessings bestowed upon us in time are a consequence of eternal election. Ἐξελέξατο, "he chose," derives from ἐκλέγω, meaning "I choose" or, more aptly, "I call out." In the context of election, it signifies the selection of one individual from among others. We will explore the various meanings of this term in the dogmatic part. In this instance, it means the choosing of some while passing over others.

2. The Object of Election: "us" (ἡμᾶς). The reference encompasses the apostle Paul and the Ephesian believers, signifying not every

individual but specifically those who believe. It is not a vague and indiscriminate selection but a deliberate choice of specific individuals, including the saints residing in Ephesus, those who believe in Christ Jesus (Eph. 1:1).

3. The Foundation of Election: "in him" (ἐν αὐτῷ). This implies those who are encompassed in Christ, united with Him, counted as part of Him. Just as, through the natural covenant, all humanity was counted as being in the first Adam (Rom. 5: 12ff.), here they are in Christ as the foundation. In Him, all the promises of God are affirmed (2 Cor. 1:20). As stated in 1 Corinthians 1:30, "From Him," signifying God, "you are in Christ Jesus, who became for us wisdom from God." Similarly, Philippians 3:9 emphasizes being found "in Him," not relying on one's own righteousness. This is not because Christ is the cause of election itself, but because He is the meritorious cause of all the saving benefits following election. The elect are "in Him" not because they preexisted in Him before election, or because they were foreseen as being in Him, but in order that, through election, they would come to be in Christ through faith.

4. The Time of Election, or its Eternal Nature: "before the foundations of the world were laid" (πρὸ καταβολῆς κόσμου). The term καταβάλλεσθαι denotes the act of laying a foundation, applied to a house and, metaphorically, to the world. Καταβολὴ refers to the beginning of the world. Consequently, this phrase signifies eternity or an election made from eternity. Anything preceding the world's creation is considered eternal, as time came into existence with the world. Anything preceding time is situated in eternity, described in Hebrew as □□□and, □□□□ as seen in Micah 5:2, "from of old," signifying "from days of

eternity."

5. The Immediate Purpose of Election: "that we should be holy and blameless before him in love" (εἶναι ἡμᾶς ἁγίους καὶ ἀμώμους κατενώπιον αὐτοῦ ἐν ἀγάπῃ). This denotes the goal or effect to which we were elected by God. It does not encompass every effect but specifically the outcome achieved in this life. In other instances, salvation (2 Thess. 2:13) and glory (Eph. 1:6) are described as effects of election, but here, the emphasis is solely on the subordinate end. It is "that we should be holy." The text does not say "because we were holy" or "because He foresaw our holiness," dispelling any notion that we were elected due to foreseen holiness or faith, or that foreknowledge served as the cause of election.

Furthermore, the ultimate aim of election includes:

a. Holiness (ἅγιοι): This denotes being inclined towards holiness and diligently pursuing it. Those who have been elected cannot help but be holy; living impiously is inconceivable unless the omnipotent God's pursuit of His own purpose were to fail.

b. Blamelessness or Perfection: Just as sacrifices needed to be without defect ( )□□□□□□in the Old Testament, Christians, as the elect, should strive for blamelessness. Terms like ἄμωμοι, ἀμώμητοι, and ἄμεμτοι are used to describe this state in various biblical passages. One who is ἄμωμος is beyond reproach, free from vice, and truly blameless. The term μῶμος, meaning "blame," seems to have originated from the Hebrew ,□□□denoting vice or defect. Our apostle may be alluding to Song of Solomon 4:7, "You are altogether beautiful, my love, and there is no blemish or defect in you." Election intends for the elect to be blameless, partly in this life through the imputation of Christ's holiness and righteousness and partly through their zeal for perfection. However, complete perfection remains unattainable during their earthly lives. Yet, it is an aspiration they continually strive towards.

c. Love (ἐν ἀγάπῃ): These words can be construed differently. Some interpret them with ἐξελέξατο, implying that God elected in love, driven by His pure and unadulterated good pleasure. Others prefer a simpler interpretation, where love is associated with the preceding words. This interpretation signifies that holiness and blamelessness should be accompanied by love for God and neighbor. Moreover, it emphasizes that every duty arising from holiness and blamelessness must stem from love.

d. Sincerity (κατενώπιον αὐτοῦ, "in His sight"): This aspect implies steadfastness and perseverance in holiness and love, akin to Psalm 102:28. It also conveys sincerity and candor. Being holy and blameless is not a mere facade before people, as hypocrites often display (Matt. 6:5; 23:5), but it primarily reflects an authentic, unblemished state before God (2 Cor. 1:12).

B. Predestination, also in a stricter sense, signifies the destination of the means for those who have been elected to reach their ultimate goal, which is eternal salvation. Concerning this predestination, the following is taught:

1. The act, in relation to its object: προορίσας ἡμᾶς, "having predestined us." Ὁρίζειν, derived from ὅρος, meaning "boundary," signifies defining, determining, or decreeing, and προορίζειν means predetermining or predestining to a specific purpose or goal. This conveys the idea that just as God separated us through election for a particular end, He also predetermined to provide us with the appropriate and fitting means to achieve that end.

2. The means: εἰς υἱοθεσίαν διὰ Χριστοῦ εἰς αὐτόν, "for adoption through Christ to himself." These words appear to suggest a threefold means:

a. The benefit: υἱοθεσία, "adoption," which encompasses not only sanctification but also our entire communion with Christ in justification, adoption, sanctification, and glorification. This broader understanding is implied in John 1:12. We have been predestined for this entire communion as the means through which the praise of God's glorious grace is manifested.

b. Redemption through Christ: διὰ Ἰησοῦ Χριστοῦ, "through Jesus Christ." This can be limited to the preceding benefit of adoption, signifying that we obtain adoption through Christ when we apprehend Him by faith (John 1:12). Alternatively, it can be extended to encompass the entire work of redemption accomplished through Christ's satisfaction, merit, and intercession. Without Christ, we cannot obtain salvation (Acts 4:12; John 14:6), nor can God receive the glory of His mercy. The apostle will elaborate on this redemption more extensively in verse 7.

c. Union with Christ: εἰς αὐτόν, "to Himself." This goes beyond God's glory, as mentioned in Proverbs 16:4 and Romans 11:36. Instead, εἰς αὐτόν indicates our union with Christ, achieved through the gathering of us to Him, primarily through the act of calling, which unites us with Christ through faith.

1. The guiding principle, or rather the motivating cause: κατὰ τὴν εὐδοκίαν τοῦ θελήματος αὐτοῦ, "according to the good pleasure of His will," and therefore, not based on merits or foreseen faith. Εὐδοκία, or in Hebrew, □□□□and " ,□□□good pleasure," is also related to reprobation, as evident from Matthew 11:25–26. Yet, when it signifies benevolence toward its object, it properly pertains to election. Additionally, εὐδοκία is a term unique to the Scriptures, coined by the Septuagint translators to render the Hebrew .□□□□θελήματος αὐτοῦ, "of His will," is added to convey that it happened in a way that pleased His will. "Will" refers to something more general, which also extends to the reprobate, while εὐδοκία typically designates the kind of will

accompanied by benevolence, from which election originates.

2. The ultimate purpose: εἰς ἔπαινον τῆς δόξης τῆς χάριτος αὐτοῦ, "to the praise of the glory of His grace." For some, ἔπαινος τῆς δόξης means "glorious praise," where the genitive serves as an adjective, following the Hebrew style. Others distinguish honor, praise, and glory so that "to honor" is associated with any good quality, "to praise" signifies a more excellent quality, and "to glory" denotes the most excellent quality, as we have explained elsewhere, in Book 2, Chapter 22, concerning the glory of God, in the exegetical part. There is an addition of ἔπαινος τῆς χάριτος, "the praise of His grace," because grace is the proper aim of election, just as avenging justice pertains to reprobation. However, there is a distinction: in election, grace is regarded as an end, albeit a subordinate one, whereas in reprobation, the just condemnation is seen merely as the means by which God achieves His ultimate purpose, the manifestation of justice. "The glory of grace" is not mentioned only because it is the specific end of election but also because it is its supreme end.

The Theological Aspect
It is demonstrated that election exists
III. Therefore, through this scripture and numerous others, it becomes as evident as the noonday sun that God, by His eternal decree, selected certain individuals by name from among humanity, who were created and had fallen in Adam. He chose them for their ultimate blessedness, where His mercy would shine forth in all its glory (Rom. 8:29–30; 9:11, 15–16; 1 Thess. 1:4; 5:9; 1 Peter 1:2; 2 John 1; Matt. 20:16; 24:22; etc.). As nothing unfolds in time that God has not eternally ordained to occur (Eph. 1:11; Acts 15:18), and given His specific predestining counsel to oversee the eternal fate of humanity, as expounded

in the previous chapter, there is no room for reasonable doubt, nor is it reasonably doubted, that eternal election indeed exists.

What is meant by the term election?

IV. Furthermore, the term "election" sometimes signifies the preordination of individuals to certain roles, whether in the political realm (1 Sam. 10:24; Ps. 78:70) or within the church (Luke 6:13; John 6:70). At times, it denotes the choice of an entire nation, to which God delivered laws, statutes, and unique demonstrations of His love (Deut. 4:37; 7:7, 15; Rom. 11:5). It can also refer to the chosen individuals themselves (Rom. 11:7), the separation that occurs in time based on the eternal decree, namely, effectual calling (Ps. 4:3; John 15:16, 19; 1 Cor. 1:27–28). However, for the most part, it signifies God's eternal decree concerning the salvation of individual believers, as evidenced by the passages mentioned in the previous section, along with Romans 8:33; Luke 18:7; Revelation 17:14; 2 Peter 1:10, and others.

The Nature of Election

V. In essence, election is the predestination of specific individuals whose eternal salvation serves as a means to display the glory of divine mercy. Since it is synonymous with predestination, the concepts discussed in the previous chapter regarding predestination are equally applicable to election.

The Four Aspects of Election

VI. Furthermore, while election is, in God's perspective, a singular and profoundly uncomplicated act, from our human standpoint, it unfolds in four distinct acts or stages, which also encompass the acts of predestination:

1. The purpose of revealing the magnificence of God's mercy through the free blessedness of individuals who have the potential to be created and to fall: "to the praise of his glorious grace" (Eph. 1:6); "in order to make known the riches of his glory toward vessels of mercy, which he prepared for glory"

(Rom. 9:23); "He chose you from the beginning for salvation" (2 Thess. 2:13).

2. The decision to create and permit the fall, thereby providing a suitable context to manifest His mercy, ultimately preparing vessels of mercy for glory (Rom. 9:23).

3. The selection and separation of specific individuals in whose blessedness He will visibly display the glory of His mercy: "The Lord knows who are his" (2 Tim. 2:19). This third act comprises three elements: (a) love, distinguishing it from the act of reprobation—"Jacob I have loved, but Esau I have hated" (Rom. 9:13); (b) love directed toward the highest and supernatural good, specifically the love through which He predestined them for glory beforehand (Rom. 9:23): "I have loved you with an everlasting love; therefore I have drawn you in mercy" (Jer. 31:3); (c) love with the aspect of segregation from others, where the virtual intention to confer that good is contained (Rom. 9:1–3; John 17:6; 1 Cor. 1:26–27).

4. The intention to prepare and direct the means by which the elect are led to their ultimate salvation, to which first redemption through Christ is aimed, followed by the application of redemption through faith (John 6:37; 2 Thess. 2:13). This act, as previously mentioned, is particularly referred to as predestination (Eph. 1:5; Rom. 8:29), mirroring the earlier act referred to as election. Consequently, it is sometimes stated that predestination occurs according to His purpose (Eph. 1:11), sometimes His purpose according to election (Rom. 9:11), and at times election according to the purpose and counsel of His will (Eph. 1:5).

Furthermore, it should be noted that these acts are accompanied by a certain divine knowledge in the mind of God, through which He most certainly knows those who will inherit eternal life. For this reason, election itself is sometimes referred to as foreknowledge (Rom. 8:29).

The Nature of the Object of Election

VII. Having carefully considered these acts of election, it is unnecessary to reiterate what we discussed in the previous chapter concerning the object of election. In a broader sense, if we include the two preceding acts, the object of election encompasses humanity, capable of being created and capable of falling. In a stricter sense, when considering the last two acts, it involves humanity as already created and fallen. Therefore, it would be more precise to state that the object of predestination is humanity capable of being created and capable of falling, while the object of election, as well as reprobation, pertains to humanity as created and fallen.

The Object of Election: The Whole Mystical Christ

VIII. It is crucial to recognize that the object of election encompasses the entirety of the mystical Christ, which includes Christ and all His followers. We are said to be elected in Christ (Eph. 1:4), predestined in Him (v. 5), accepted in the Beloved (v. 6), to have redemption in Him (v. 7), to obtain an inheritance in Him (v. 11), to be called and sealed in Him (v. 13). It is stated that God was pleased to gather all things in Christ (v. 10), just as we all sinned and perished in the first Adam, and we are all restored in the second Adam (Rom. 5:12). However, it is important to understand that Christ, when considered personally in this election, is Himself the head and the one entirely blameless and righteous (Rom. 5:18–19), while humans, as members in Him (Eph. 1:4), are fallen and in need of redemption.

How Christ Is Involved in Election

IX. From this perspective, it becomes evident how Christ is intertwined in the work of election:

1. As God, along with the Father and the Holy Spirit, He is the author of election, even though, from the perspective of divine economy in the Scriptures, the work of election is often attributed to the Father.

2. As the Mediator, responsible for procuring salvation for the elect, Christ can be viewed either as the instrumental cause, whereby salvation is the result of God saving us through Christ, or as the principal cause, since this salvation is a benefit bestowed upon humanity. Consequently, Christ is referred to as the author and perfecter of our faith (Heb. 12:2). In the first act of election, or the purpose of manifesting mercy, Christ is involved as the means of gratuitous beatification. In the final act, He is the principal cause of the beatification of the elect.

The Causes of Election

X. Christ, the Mediator, is not the meritorious cause of election, as He is of the salvation destined for the elect. Election is the act of choosing the elect themselves, and through election, Christ was designated as the Mediator (1 Peter 1:20; Isa. 42:1). Neither faith, good works, nor any foreseen deeds were motivating causes for God to elect. (1) Election, like any decree, does not have causes in the same sense. (2) Faith and good works could not have been foreseen as future events without a prior divine decree. (3) Faith and good works originate from election as their primary source, a consistent theme in Scripture, which we will explore further in the later sections.

The Primary Cause of Election: The Entire Trinity

The Sole Impelling Cause: His Divine Good Pleasure

XI. Therefore, the triune God is the ultimate cause of election (1 Peter 1:2): the Father (Eph. 1:3–4; John 6:37; 17:2), the Son (John 13:18; 15:16, 19), and the Holy Spirit, evident through His sealing and divine works (Acts 13:2; Eph. 1:13; John 3:6; 1 Cor. 6:11). No other leading cause is apparent other than God's pure and unadulterated good pleasure (Eph. 1:5; Rom. 9:16–18, 21–23; Matt. 11:25–26; Luke 12:32).

The Ultimate Goal: The Glory of His Grace

The Supreme End: The glory of God, but not a general glory as in every decree, rather a distinct glory, that of grace and mercy (Eph. 1:6; Rom. 9:23). Serving as a subordinate end is the gratuitous salvation of the elect. This is why the elect are appointed for salvation (1 Thess. 5:9) and prepared beforehand for glory (Rom. 9:23). The means to achieve this subordinate end include faith and union and communion with Christ in justification, adoption, sanctification, and all aspects of salvation. It is said that the end of faith is the salvation of our souls (1 Peter 1:9), and that we were elected to be holy (Eph. 1:4), and predestined to be conformed to the image of the Son of God (Rom. 8:29). Election is referred to as "the foreknowledge of God the Father in the sanctification of the Spirit" (1 Peter 1:2). Although these means are coordinated with each other in achieving this end rather than being subordinate, they collectively contribute to salvation because individually, they do not produce the supreme end of election.

The Nature of Election

XII. Concerning its attributes, election is, firstly, eternal – existing before the confines of time (Eph. 1:4). There is no temporal election distinct from the calling, by which we are actually elected into ourselves (1 Cor. 1:26–28). It does not emerge only after faith, nor does it transpire at the moment of death, let alone after death.

1. Absolute, Immutable, and Certain

XIII. Secondly, election is absolute, unchanging, and certain. It stands as the unshakable foundation of God, bearing the seal of His knowledge, for God not only knows the quantity but also the identity of those who are His (2 Tim. 2:19). "For those whom He foreknew He also predestined," as the Scriptures affirm (Rom. 8:29). It is stated that what

God has purposed according to election remains firm (Rom. 9:11), and that "the election" attains salvation (Rom. 11:7).

The Book of Life

This concept is echoed in the reference to "the book of life" (Isa. 4:3; Phil. 4:3; Rev. 13:8; 17:8; 20:12, 15; 21:27). Although the term "the book of God" sometimes signifies God's common providence (Ps. 139:16; Dan. 7:10; 12:1; Mal. 3:16), other times it pertains to the record of those living on the earth (Ps. 69:28), which may align with Moses' understanding in Exodus 32:32. At times, it denotes the book of shared predestination (Rev. 20:12), shedding light on how one might be blotted out from the book of God. Thus, the number of the elect is definite and fixed, unalterable by increase or decrease. A shadow of this certainty can be seen in the census of the Israelites in the wilderness, which, when conducted again, yielded the same number of heads both times, with a remarkable consistency (Ex. 38:26 and Num. 1:46). This image is, it seems, invoked and followed by the Holy Spirit in Revelation 7:4.

The Assurance of Individual Election

XIV. It is not only God who is certain of those who belong to Him through this book, but also each of the elect. While they may not always be absolutely certain, ordinary indicators can lead them to believe that their own names are inscribed in the book of election (Luke 10:20; 1:4). To this end, they are exhorted to confirm their calling and election (2 Peter 1:10).

The Elenctic Inquiry

1. Are There Multiple Elections?

XV. First, it is essential to address the question of whether the Scriptures speak of multiple elections. Various groups, including Pelagians, Socinians, semi-Pelagians, Jesuits, Remonstrants, and others, who are joined by Lutherans on this matter, introduce numerous distinctions to challenge the scriptural doctrine of election. They propose several types of election.

According to their perspective, there is: (1) an election of state, such as "I will save all believers, I will condemn all unbelievers." In their view, this election is eternal, absolute, unchanging, and universal. (2) There is an election of particular individuals, for instance, the election of Peter. In their understanding, this election, as far as its eternality is concerned, is conditional, mutable, and incomplete. From eternity, it is decreed in this manner: Peter will be saved if he chooses to believe. (3) Finally, there is a temporal election, which can be either non-conclusive, like "I will save Peter, whom I currently see believing, if he continues in faith," or conclusive, occurring at the moment of death or even after death when perseverance through free choice has been accomplished.

Refutation of Spurious Elections

The Reformed position, while acknowledging that the term "election" signifies various aspects concerning persons, ends, and means, maintains in harmony with Scripture the existence of only one genuine election while rejecting the spurious elections proposed by our adversaries. Specifically:

1. Scripture dismisses the notion of a general and indefinite election of state because it consistently ties election to specific persons (Acts 13:48; Rom. 8:29–30; 9:11; Eph. 1:4–6). We have thoroughly addressed and refuted this concept in Book 3, Chapter 1, §XXXII.

2. Scripture does not permit an election of persons that is conditional and incomplete, as it teaches that God ordained both the end and every means through a single, simple act (2 Thess. 2:13; Rom. 8:29–30; Eph. 1:4–6). We have also dismantled this form of election in the cited chapter, §XXX.

3. There is no trace in Scripture of a non-peremptory, variable

election that occurs at or after death. To the contrary, the purpose of election is portrayed as firm (2 Tim. 2:19; Heb. 6:17; Rom. 9:11; 11:28–29). We have addressed the mutability of this kind of election in the cited chapter, §XXXIII, and its temporality in §XXIX. Since these objections have already been refuted in those passages, there is no need to revisit them here.

The Question of Universal Election and Diverse Opinions

XVI. Secondly, we inquire whether there exists any form of universal election. Origen once proposed that not only every human being but even the devils themselves were elected to salvation. He suggested that after enduring penalties commensurate with their sins in hell for some time, eventually each one of them would enter into heaven. This perspective was also shared by Francesco Pucci, the Italian Socinian, as well as by the Swiss theologian Samuel Huber. Huber, originally a Reformed preacher, later became a Lutheran ecclesiastic but was subsequently removed from ministry by the Lutherans due to this very belief. Additionally, some Arminian Socinianizers, such as Sebastian Castellio in his Four Dialogues, adopted a similar viewpoint.

Lutherans make a distinction between a proper use and an improper, or catachrestic, use of the term "election." They claim that if election is understood catachrestically to refer to God's benevolent will and universal love toward all or to the negation of the reprobating decree or to God's decree to create all in Adam for eternal life and renew all in Christ for eternal life or to the universal offer of means of salvation to all, then, according to them, it is acceptable to speak of election as universal. However, they deny that election, in its proper and scriptural meaning, is universal. They assert that God's counsel concerning the salvation of individuals can be viewed either within His antecedent will, in which case it is universal, or within His consequent will, in which case it becomes particular due to the foreseen final unbelief of certain individuals. Therefore, they construct a universal predestination based on three principles: (1) a universal divine will to save all, (2) universal redemption through Christ, and (3) a universal calling. However, not all are saved through this universal predestination because they do not will to believe. This concept is elaborated in Johann Gerhard's Loci Theologici (Volume 2, Chapter 10, regarding election and reprobation) and Hafenreffer's Loci Communes.

Pelagians and Pelagianizers, driven by their inclination toward universal grace at least in terminology, do not embrace universal election, as it entails a connection to reprobation, which they do accept in terms of the word. Nevertheless, they do fully accept the substance of universal election when they teach that God desires the salvation of each and every person, at least in His antecedent will. We have previously rejected this viewpoint common to both Pelagians and Lutherans in Book 2, Chapter 15, §XXX (also see the preceding paragraphs). We will now consider the former opinion of Huber and Castellio, which upholds an absolute, universal election.

The Reformed Perspective with Explanations

The Reformed position does not allow for any form of universal election for the following reasons:

1. Scripture contains no mention whatsoever of universal election.

2. On the contrary, it consistently teaches particular election (Matt. 20:16; 22:14; John 15:19; 17:6; Rom. 8:29; 9:13, 15, 18, 22; 1 Thess. 5:9), with no counter-examples.

3. Election implies choosing from among several options, preferring one over another, or accepting one while rejecting another (Deut. 7:7; John 15:19). Therefore, universal election is a contradiction.

4. Universal election would negate the concept of reprobation, which Scripture opposes (Rom. 9:18, 22; Jude 4; Prov. 16:4; Matt. 25:41).

5. The elect are said to be recorded in the book of life (Luke 10:20; Phil. 4:3), which is explicitly denied for those who will perish (Rev. 13:8; 17:8).

6. Adoption is attributed to the elect (Eph. 1:5), which is neither stated nor can be applied to all.

7. The elect are said to be foreknown, implying forelove (Rom. 8:29; 11:2; 2 Tim. 2:19; 1 Peter 1:2; Ps. 1:6), a quality denied for the reprobate (Matt. 7:23).

8. The elect are those destined to believe (Eph. 1:5), which is not applicable to the reprobate.

9. This view would result in the perishing of many among the elect, contrary to Paul (Rom. 8:29).

10. Universal election, if proposed, would either be settled or unsettled. If the former, then each and every individual would be saved, contradicting previous points and, specifically, Matthew 25. If the latter, it would imply either a change in God, which is contrary to His immutability (Mal. 3:6) and His unchanging counsel (Isa. 46:10; Heb. 6:17), or a change by another, which is impossible since the one altering the plans of another must be prior, superior, and more powerful.

Responses to Objections

It is not valid to argue as follows:

1. That the decree of mercy, coinciding with election, is universal based on Romans 11:31–32. The passage does not state "on

each and every person" but "on all," implying every class of people or every kind, including both Jews and Gentiles. This interpretation is evident from the broader context and supported by Paul's explanations in Galatians 3:22 and Romans 3:22.

2. Using John 3:16, "God so loved the world...". In this context, "the world" refers to all believers, not just those from the Jewish community as it was under the old covenant but also from all Gentiles (Rom. 11:11–12).

3. Referring to passages like 1 Tim. 2:4, "God wills all to be saved," and similar ones. Responses include: (a) "God wills all to be saved" applies to those of all kinds, including both kings and subjects. If Paul intended "all" to mean every individual, he would be commanding us to pray for every person, which John does not permit (1 John 5:16) and Christ does not do (John 17:9). (b) "He does not will the death of the sinner" who repents but does will it otherwise (1 Sam. 2:25; Prov. 1:26). (c) "He does not will any to perish" among believers but wills "all to come to repentance."

The Nature of Election: Foreseen or God's Good Pleasure

Now, let us consider the question of whether there is a cause or reason for election beyond the divine good pleasure.

Various theological perspectives have been presented throughout history:

- Pelagians and many papists argue for foreseen merits.

- Socinians and Remonstrants reject foreseen merits but propose foreseen faith and good works.

- Lutherans uphold foreseen faith, often coupled with the merit of Christ.

- Augustine and the Reformed, following the Scriptures, firmly assert the divine good pleasure as the sole cause.

We, in line with Augustine and the Reformed tradition, maintain the divine good pleasure as the exclusive cause of election for several compelling reasons:

1. All divine decrees, especially predestination, are eternal, self-determined, and absolute, as demonstrated in preceding chapters.

2. Scripture consistently attributes election solely to the good pleasure of God (Matt. 11:26; Luke 12:32; 2 Tim. 1:9; Rom. 9:11–12), even describing it as an act of grace (Rom. 11:5).

3. We are elected not because of our faith and works but to faith and sanctification (Eph. 1:4; Rom. 8:29; John 15:16). Consequently,

4. Faith, sanctification, and perseverance are the fruits of election (Acts 13:48; John 6:37; 8:47).

5. Faith and good works can only exist in the future as a result of the decree of election.

6. If our election depended on foreknowledge of our faith, works, or perseverance, these qualities would either arise from us (contradicting the apostle in 1 Cor. 4:7) or God would have decreed to grant them through election.

Challenging these points, some have raised objections:

1. They argue that the predestined are explicitly referred to as foreknown (Rom. 8:29; 1 Peter 1:1–2). In response, we clarify that being foreknown means being foreloved, not predestined

due to foreseen faith (Ps. 1:6; Matt. 7:23).

2. It is suggested that no one could be loved by God for election without being considered in Christ through faith (Heb. 11:6). However, we contend that God's love includes providing Christ (John 3:16) and faith in Christ (Phil. 1:29), which, in turn, leads us to please Him (Heb. 11:6).

3. They point to passages that mention being elected in Christ (Eph. 1:4). We explain that we are not described as already existing in Him but as those who will be, just as we are also spoken of as redeemed and called in Him (Eph. 1:7, 11, 13) to gain salvation through Christ.

4. Some argue that justification and salvation result from faith, and thus, election must also depend on faith. We clarify that while we are elected to be justified by faith and obtain salvation, faith itself is not the immediate cause of election.

Is Christ the Foundation of Election?

Now, let us consider the fourth question: Is Christ, as the Mediator, the foundation of election, particularly its meritorious cause? This matter has been disputed, with the Remonstrants and Lutherans contending that Christ serves as this foundation. It is essential to explore this concept and clarify our stance.

While there is no scriptural reference explicitly stating that Christ is the foundation of election (as He is of salvation, as affirmed in 1 Cor. 3:11 and Eph. 2:20), we do not deny that it can be expressed in the sense that He is the foundation of its execution. This perspective arises because God ordained to dispense the salvation of election exclusively through Christ. However, we consistently deny that Christ is the meritorious cause of election itself.

Our reasons for maintaining this position are as follows:

1. Every divine decree, especially predestination, including election, is independent and devoid of a cause, reason, or anything other than the good pleasure of the electing God.

2. Christ is an effect of election, serving as the instrument through which God chose to save the elect (Isa. 42:1; Matt. 12:18; 1 Peter 1:20).

3. In the sequence of election, Christ and His merit do not hold the primary place but the secondary one (John 3:16; Rom. 8:29–30; 2 Tim. 1:9). The focus is not on obtaining God's election through Christ's merit, as is the case with redemption and reconciliation, but rather on receiving it through God's grace and mercy (Eph. 1; Col. 1; etc.).

However, objections have been raised against this standpoint:

1. It is argued that we are elected in Christ (Eph. 1:4). In response, we clarify that this does not mean being elected because of Christ, but being elected to obtain salvation through Christ and faith in Christ. The term "in" may be understood as "through," as evident from subsequent verses and parallel passages (1 Thess. 5:9; 2 Thess. 2:13–14).

2. Some contend that our position implies that Christ is not the foundation of our salvation (1 Cor. 3:11) and, consequently, that the salvation of individuals is not grounded in Christ. To this, we reply that there is a significant distinction between the divine action that destines us to salvation and salvation itself, such that the One called the foundation and author of the latter (Heb. 2:10) should also immediately be regarded as such for the former.

3. It is suggested that it contradicts divine justice to love and elect

anyone outside of Christ. Our response is that God cannot love anyone outside of Christ with the love of complacency, wherein He finds pleasure (Heb. 11:6). However, it is not impossible for God to express benevolent love toward someone by willing to grant them Christ and faith in Christ (John 3:16).

Are Election to Glory and Election to Grace Equally Absolute?

Now, let us consider the fifth question: Are election to glory and election to grace equally absolute? Are they both entirely dependent on God's sovereign choice, or do they involve foreseen factors? This issue has been a point of contention, with various theological perspectives.

Some, such as the semi-Pelagians, Arminians, and Jesuits, advocate for the idea that the entirety of election should be based on foreseen factors. The Jesuits, in particular, suggest that election should be determined by foreseen merits. In contrast, Augustine, in alignment with Scripture and the Dominicans, asserts that the entirety of election is absolute. Ambrosius Catharinus at the Council of Trent articulated that election to grace was absolute, but election to glory was based on foreseen merits.

As Reformed theologians, we align ourselves with the Scriptures and Augustine, affirming that the entirety of election is absolute, whether it pertains to election to glory or to grace. We maintain this stance based on several reasons:

1. The Scriptures themselves describe election as "gratuitous" or stemming from grace (Rom. 11:5). This description explicitly excludes any works or merits as the basis for election (Rom. 11:6; Eph. 2:8–9; 1 Cor. 1:28–29; 4:7; Rom. 3:27).

2. We are elected so that we may perform good works (Eph. 1:4; John 15:16). Therefore, our election cannot be based on foreseen works.

3. The process of calling, which is a direct consequence of election

(Rom. 8:28–30) and the cause of good works, occurs absolutely and independently, devoid of any foreseen factors (2 Tim. 1:9–10; John 15:16, 19; Eph. 2:8–9).

4. The entirety of election is attributed to God's good pleasure alone (Eph. 1:4–5, 11; Rom. 9:11, 18; Luke 12:32; 2 Tim. 1:9).

It is important to address objections raised against this position:

1. Some argue that we typically choose something because it is better, especially when selecting a few items from a multitude. Accordingly, they contend that God elected those who appeared better, endowed with virtues and works. However, we clarify that election can occur either because something is better (based on merit) or so that it may become better (based on grace). Creatures may elect based on merit, but the Creator elects based on grace.

2. Another objection posits that since glory is given based on merits, election must have been decreed on account of merits as well. We reject this argument, emphasizing the distinction between election to glory and the glory itself. These are different aspects: one pertains to God's divine action, and the other to the creature's good.

3. It is suggested that our zeal for good works makes us more certain of our election (2 Peter 1:10; 2 Tim. 2:20). However, this does not imply that we were elected to glory on account of our works.

Is the Number of the Elect Invariable?

Now, let us explore the sixth question: Is the number of the elect entirely unchanging? Or can it vary based on human choices and actions? This topic has sparked diverse opinions among theologians.

The Socinians, Pelagians, Remonstrants, and Jesuits, driven by their emphasis on the independent and self-determined nature of free choice, deny the invariability of the number of the elect. Among Lutherans, there is a lack of consensus, as some argue that it is invariable according to divine foreknowledge, while others assert that it remains invariable with respect to the elect, who have the capacity to believe or not believe.

Orthodox theologians maintain that the number of the elect is, indeed, invariable. They argue this on the basis of the following reasons:

1. Every decree of God, including the decree of predestination, is immutable, as discussed in previous chapters.

2. Through election, God infallibly knows both the quantity and identity of those who belong to Him (2 Tim. 2:19; John 13:18; Rom. 8:29; 11:2, 29).

However, objections are raised against this view:

1. Some argue that God wills the salvation of every individual (1 Tim. 2:4), implying that the number of the elect is not fixed. It is crucial to clarify that the antecedent assumption is false and not explicitly stated by the apostle.

2. It is suggested that the elect can potentially become reprobate, citing passages such as (a) 1 Corinthians 9:27, where Paul expresses concern about becoming reprobate. However, in this context, "reprobate" is not in opposition to eternal election but signifies moral blamelessness or irreprehensibility. (b) Matthew 11:21 is cited, where it is suggested that if the inhabitants of Tyre and Sidon had the same opportunities, they would have repented. This passage does not address the transition from reprobate to elect but emphasizes the greater culpability of those who reject Christ despite having more opportunities for salvation. (c) Romans 11:23 mentions God's ability to graft

the Jews back in, but it does not imply that the reprobate can become elect; it speaks of the restoration of the Jewish race.

3. The idea that someone can be blotted out of the book of life (Ex. 32:33; Ps. 69:28; Rev. 3:5; 22:19) is also raised as an objection. However, these passages do not refer to the book of eternal election but rather to different contexts. Revelation 3:5, for example, promises a secure and unchanging blessing to those who overcome, akin to the assurance found in Philippians 1:6. Revelation 22:19 presents a conditional warning that does not imply the actual erasure of someone from the book of life, as God has already decreed and foreknown that none of the elect will commit such an act.

These objections will be further addressed in our discussion on the perseverance of the elect.

Can a Believer Be Certain of Their Election?

In our final inquiry, we ponder whether a true believer, through ordinary means, can be absolutely certain of their own election. This question has stirred diverse responses among theologians.

The Pelagians, Papists, Socinians, and Remonstrants adamantly deny this certainty, arguing that the human will maintains perpetual and independent indifference. On the other hand, the Lutherans do affirm it but introduce the caveat that the truly elect can entirely fall away, which leads them to withhold this affirmation.

The orthodox position, rooted in both Scripture and tradition, firmly asserts that a believer can indeed be certain of their own election. This assurance is supported by several compelling reasons:

1. The elect are instructed to make their calling and election sure (2 Peter 1:10). This command implies the possibility of certainty, not in God but within themselves.

2. They possess within themselves the marks of election and the accompanying signs of salvation (Heb. 6:9). Believers can be certain of their faith, which is inseparably linked to salvation and, consequently, to election (2 Tim. 1:12; John 3:16).

3. The presence of the Holy Spirit, who serves as the seal and guarantee of our inheritance (2 Cor. 1:22; Eph. 1:13–14; 4:30), bears witness with our spirit (Rom. 8:16).

4. Numerous examples of this certainty can be found in Scripture (Ps. 23:1, 6; Rom. 8:38; Gal. 2:20; 2 Tim. 4:8; 2 Cor. 5:1; Gal. 4:6).

Contrary to these arguments, objections are raised:

1. Some argue that we have not been privy to God's counsel (Rom. 11:34) or ascended into heaven (Rom. 10:6) to examine the book of life. Nevertheless, we can deduce, through a posteriori reasoning from the bestowed blessings that God grants exclusively to the elect, that we have been chosen by Him.

2. It is suggested that this certainty might lead to carelessness, pride, carnality, and laziness. However, these accusations are unfounded (2 Peter 1:10–11; 1 John 3:3).

3. The prevalence of exhortations to fear in Scripture (Ps. 2:11–12; Phil. 2:11–12) is cited as evidence against such certainty. Yet, this fear should be understood as filial reverence toward God as our Father (Heb. 12:28), not as doubt regarding election and salvation.

4. The argument that some have fallen from faith (1 Tim. 1:19–20) is raised. However, this pertains to a profession of faith (Rom. 1:8) or a type of transient or superficial faith (Matt.

13:20–21; 1 Cor. 13:2).

The Practical Aspect
Divine election has profound implications for our understanding of God's glory and authority.

1. **Manifestation of God's Glory and Sovereignty**: The decree of election vividly showcases the glory of God. It underscores His supreme authority and sovereignty, likened to a potter's authority over clay. Just as the potter shapes vessels according to his will, God, in His sovereignty, forms vessels of both wrath and grace, electing or passing over individuals according to His divine purpose (Rom. 9:22; Jer. 18:6; Matt. 20:15).

   ○ In the practical realm of our faith, we should contemplate how God's sovereignty plays a pivotal role in our lives. It's a reminder that He is the ultimate authority, orchestrating His divine plan with unwavering control.

2. **Revelation of His Mercy**: Election also magnifies God's mercy. We are described as vessels of mercy, chosen to praise His glorious grace (Rom. 9:23; Eph. 1:6). The unparalleled display of His mercy shines most brilliantly in election. He chooses individuals from among sinners, His own enemies, purely out of His goodwill, without any merit or worthiness on our part. It's a grace-driven act, where God freely gives His Son and the Holy Spirit to us, bestowing faith upon us without expecting anything in return (Rom. 11:36; John 3:16).

   ○ This aspect of election encourages us to marvel at the depth of God's mercy, motivating us to live lives marked by gratitude and praise for His unmerited favor.

3. **Demonstration of Divine Wisdom**: God's wisdom is on full

display in election. He meticulously arranges and links together the most fitting means to achieve His divine purpose (Rom. 8:29–30; Eph. 1:4–6; 2 Thess. 2:13). His wisdom harmonizes mercy and justice, particularly exemplified in the way He reconciles these attributes through the sacrifice of Christ (Rom. 3:25). This leads the apostle to exclaim, "Oh, the richness of God's wisdom and knowledge! His judgments are unfathomable, and His ways are beyond our comprehension! Who can claim to understand the mind of the Lord? Who could ever presume to be His counselor?" (Romans 11:33–34).

To what purpose, then, does God manifest these virtues in election? It is so that we may not only recognize them but also proclaim them with a devout declaration, saying, "To Him be glory forever. Amen" (Romans 11:36).

1. It stirs us to seek assurance of our election

Furthermore, as a second point, it encourages us to seek and attain assurance regarding our own election. We should diligently strive to make it certain (2 Peter 1:10), examining ourselves to ensure that we are not rejected (reprobi, ἀδόκιμοι, 2 Corinthians 13:5).

Motivations

This pursuit of assurance accomplishes several essential things: (1) It ignites our zeal for holiness (2 Peter 1:10), motivating us to lead lives characterized by holiness and blamelessness in His love (Ephesians 1:4). (2) It guards us against falling into apostasy and sin (2 Peter 1:10). (3) It abundantly prepares us for an entrance into the eternal kingdom of our Lord and Savior Jesus Christ (2 Peter 1:11). (4) It strengthens and fortifies us in times of adversity (Romans 8:35, 38–39). (5) It grants us easier access to God (Hebrews 10:22). In a word, (6) it offers us a taste of heaven while we are still on earth (Ephesians 1:3–4; Hebrews 11:1). One effort addresses two objectives: when we secure our calling, we also secure our election (2 Peter 1:10). Those whom God foreknew, He predestined, and those He predestined, He called (Romans 8:29–30). Furthermore, our calling becomes sure when we add virtue to our faith, and knowledge to virtue, and so forth (2 Peter 1:5–6).

The certainty of election is revealed through two types of signs: those belonging to God, which provide assurance, and those exhibited by us as evidence of our election. God's manifestation of election includes:

1. **Election in Time:** God's eternal election is confirmed by our calling in time. This calling separates those chosen by Him in His eternal counsel from the worldly and carnal masses. Through this calling, God prepares individuals as vessels of grace, dedicating themselves to Him (1 Corinthians 1:26–27).

2. **Reception into His Household:** Those whom God has chosen are received into His household. They are blessed to dwell in His courts, which happens through the power of His Word, the strength of His promises, and the influence of the Holy Spirit. We hear God's call, follow His guidance, and become part of His household (Psalm 65:4; 1 Thessalonians 1:4–6).

3. **Sanctification through Adversity:** God's election is revealed through the sanctification of the cross and hardships He allows His chosen ones to face. In the midst of difficulties, God pours out His love, shapes them in patience, humility, prayer, and a hatred of sin. They recognize His love even in adversity and acknowledge that it was good for them to be afflicted (Romans 5:5; Psalm 119:71; Romans 8:28–29).

These indicators make it evident that God has elected us.

On the other hand, the elect demonstrate their election through various signs:

1. **Sanctification by the Spirit:** The elect are sanctified by the

Holy Spirit, chosen to be holy and blameless in love (Ephesians 1:4; 2 Thessalonians 2:13; 1 Peter 1:2).

2. **Reflecting Christ's Virtues:** The virtues of Christ should shine throughout the lives of the elect. They were chosen in Christ to be united with Him, and His qualities, such as humility, patience, love, obedience, and contempt for the world, should be evident in their actions (Ephesians 1:4; 2 Peter 1:5–7, 10; 1 Peter 2:9).

3. **Affection for God:** Those who are blameless before God in love should reciprocate with love for God, His Word, and His commandments. They should also extend this love to fellow believers who are also chosen in Christ (Ephesians 1:4; Colossians 3:12). This love is further demonstrated when it remains steadfast in the face of adversity (Romans 8:28, 35).

4. **Spiritual Priesthood:** The elect function as a spiritual priesthood, offering themselves to God by mortifying the flesh and its worldly affections, akin to a sacrificial offering on Christ as the altar (Galatians 2:20; 5:24; 6:14).

5. **Worldly Hostility:** The world's hatred and persecution of the elect serve as a sign of their distinction from the world. Their election results in the world's enmity, as they are no longer of the world but chosen out of it (John 15:18–19).

These signs and characteristics serve as evidence of election and are reflective of God's grace and purpose in the lives of the chosen ones.

When we have attained the assurance of our election, it compels us to express our gratitude to God. As it is written, "Blessed be the Father of our Lord Jesus Christ ... who chose us ..." (Ephesians 1:3–4). We are reminded that we should always give thanks to God, beloved by the Lord,

because He has chosen us from the beginning (2 Thessalonians 2:13; 1
Thessalonians 1:2, 4).

This call to gratitude is profound because of several compelling reasons:

1. He chose us when He could have justly rejected us (Romans
   9:21).

2. He selected us from among countless others whom He passed
   by and did not choose (Romans 9:27–29; 11:3, 5, 7, 22).

3. He elected us while we were fallen, corrupt, sinful, and His
   enemies (Romans 5:8; Ezekiel 16:5–6).

4. His election was motivated solely by His pure, unadulterated
   mercy, without any expectation of gain or advantage, driven by
   His good pleasure alone (Ephesians 1:5; Matthew 11:25–26).

5. He chose us not for servitude or mere friendship with God
   but for adoption (Ephesians 1:5), justification, sanctification,
   and eternal glorification (Romans 8:30), and an imperishable
   inheritance kept in the heavens for us (1 Peter 1:4).

6. We were chosen in Christ to be redeemed by His own blood,
   united with Him, and blessed with the sharing of all His benefits. We are beloved by God through the foreknowledge of His
   Son's obedience and the sprinkling of His blood (1 Peter 1:2), so
   that we may be complete in Him (Colossians 2:10; 1 Corinthians 1:30), conformed to the image of His Son (Romans 8:29).

7. He chose us through the sanctification of the Spirit (1 Peter 1:2;
   2 Thessalonians 2:13), so that we may be regenerated, convert-
   ed, and renewed (John 3:5; Titus 3:5).

In response, we should express our gratitude to God: (1) in our hearts, by recognizing the magnitude and quality of this blessing, by understanding and valuing it, and by attributing it solely to God and His pure, unadulterated love and benevolence (Psalm 103:1–3; 116:12; Genesis 32:10); (2) with our mouths, as a chosen people, by proclaiming the virtues of the One who called us (1 Peter 2:9; Psalm 51:14); and finally, (3) through our actions, by reciprocating the love of the God who, through His pure, unadulterated love, chose us (Psalm 116:1–5). We choose God in return, becoming witnesses against ourselves that we have chosen to serve Him (Joshua 24:22; Psalm 16:5–6). Since He separated us from the world through His choice, we must, in turn, separate ourselves for Him by distancing ourselves from the world (John 15:19), not conforming to its ways (Romans 12:2), coming out of it (Revelation 18:4; Hebrews 13:13). Furthermore, because He chose us to be holy and blameless before Him in love, we should diligently pursue holiness, as we shall discuss in the following section.

Furthermore, it stirs within us a fervent zeal for holiness, supported by numerous compelling reasons:

1. The One who elected us is holy (Leviticus 11:44–45; Matthew 5:48).

2. He chose us to be a holy people, precious to Him (Deuteronomy 14:2), "a chosen race, a royal priesthood, a holy people" (1 Peter 2:9).

3. His purpose in choosing us is holiness, "that we should be holy and blameless before Him" (Ephesians 1:4), achieved through the sanctification of the Holy Spirit (2 Thessalonians 2:13; 1 Peter 1:2).

4. He chose us in Christ, the Holy One of Israel (Isaiah 10:20), whom the Father sanctified for this purpose (John 10:36), and

who sanctified Himself for us, that we too might be holy (John 17:19). In Christ, we become new creatures (2 Corinthians 5:17), created for good works, to walk in them (Ephesians 2:10).

5. His election is for us to be conformed to the image of His Son (Romans 8:29).

6. He elected us out of pure, unadulterated grace, which instructs us to deny ungodliness and worldly lusts, leading us to live moderately, righteously, and godly lives (Titus 2:12).

7. Through His election, He set us apart from the world (John 15:19), urging us to separate ourselves from worldly conformity and instead be renewed in the spirit of our minds (Romans 12:2).

To practice this zeal for holiness, we should:

1. Love God, just as He loved us by choosing us—"Those whom He foreknew ..." (Romans 8:29)—establishing a reciprocal love (Song of Solomon 2:16).

2. Love purely and gratuitously, mirroring the unmotivated love of the One who elected us. Our love for Him should be solely for His sake, without expecting anything in return.

3. Love in a way that we choose Him above all else, even in disregard and contempt for all others (Psalm 73:25), just as He disregarded countless others when choosing us.

4. Choose Him with the intention of dedicating ourselves entirely to Him, just as He dedicated His Son and all He possesses, even His very self, to us, His chosen.

5. Dedicate ourselves and all our possessions to His glory, living

and, if necessary, dying for Him (Romans 14:7–9; Philippians 1:20–21).

6. Offer our names to God as if signing them over to Him (Isaiah 44:1, 5), just as He has recorded our names in the book of life.

Fifthly, divine election provides us with a compelling argument for finding comfort in times of adversity, experiencing indescribable joy in times of favor, and resting in peaceful confidence in any circumstance. From the doctrine of election, we derive the following assurances:

1. An unwavering certainty of our eternal salvation and life, even in the face of death, because God chose us "from the beginning ... to obtain the glory of our Lord Jesus Christ" (2 Thessalonians 2:13–14; Psalm 23:6). We can be confident in God's unchanging love for us (Romans 11:2; 8:38–39).

2. Assurance of our gracious acceptance into God's household and the perpetual communion and fellowship with God: "Blessed is the one whom you have chosen and have made to draw near to yourself, that he may dwell in your courts. He will be satisfied with the good of your house, with the holiness of your temple" (Psalm 65:4; cf. Isaiah 65:13–14).

3. Confidence in divine protection during times of danger and adversity: "Fear not, for I am with you; be not dismayed, for I am your God; I have strengthened you, I am also your help, and I have upheld you by my righteous right hand. Behold, all those who are wrathful against you will be ashamed and embarrassed; they shall be as nothing, and the men who contend with you shall perish" (Isaiah 41:10–13; cf. Psalm 23:4–5; 3:5–8).

4. The assurance that even the most challenging adversities, through God's grace, will not only be softened for us (Psalm

73:26) but also work together for our ultimate good and salvation (Romans 8:28). We can even take pride in our tribulations because of the overflowing love of God in our hearts (Romans 5:2–5).

5. The certainty that despite our rejection by the world, we are chosen by God and eternally accepted by Him. Our prayers will be heard and answered: "You have not chosen me, but I have chosen you that you should go and bear fruit, so that whatever you ask the Father in my name he may give to you" (John 15:16; cf. Hebrews 4:16; 10:22).

6. The certainty that Christ, as our friend, will share with us the Father's secrets and the mysteries of His kingdom (John 15:15–16; Psalm 25:14; Genesis 18:17).

7. The assurance that on the day of judgment, all accusations against us will be dismissed, as Christ, by the decree of election, was designated as our Redeemer and Advocate. "If God is for us, who can be against us? He who did not spare his own Son but gave him up for us all, how will he not also with him graciously give us all things? Who shall bring any charge against God's elect? It is God who justifies. Who is to condemn? Christ Jesus is the one who died" (Romans 8:31–35).

All these countless benefits remain steadfast and sure for us, as long as we sincerely believe in and are persuaded of our election without hypocrisy.

Sixthly, divine election also sets forth an example for us to follow. We are not only to choose God, as we've discussed, but also to choose those whom God has elected alongside us. We have been chosen by the same love and grace, for the same purpose, in the same head, Christ, into the same mystical body, for the same union and communion with

His Son, and through the same means of salvation. Therefore, as the chosen of God, holy and beloved, let us clothe ourselves with compassion, kindness, humility, gentleness, patience, and forgiveness, just as Christ has shown to us (Colossians 3:12–13; John 15:17; 17:26). Let us not discriminate between people but extend our love even to the most marginalized, for "God has chosen the poor of this world to be rich in faith and heirs of the kingdom which he has promised to those who love him" (James 2:5; 1 Corinthians 1:27). We should be prepared to endure all things for their sake because they are dearly beloved by God, who also elected us (2 Timothy 2:10).

Seventhly, it is crucial to recognize and avoid the dangers that could not only cause us to lose the benefits of election we've discussed but also hasten our destruction. These dangers include:

1. The notion of a universal election, which suggests that every person will ultimately be saved through God's mercy. This belief undermines the importance of confirming our own election, which is essential for godliness and comfort. We have addressed this idea in detail in the earlier section.

2. The rash attempt to ascertain our election from above, trying to immediately see whether our names are written in the book of life. Such an approach is prone to disappointment and should be avoided. Instead, we should begin by examining our hearts to see if they exhibit qualities that are unmistakably connected to election. We should follow the apostolic ladder described in Romans 8:29–30, ascending step by step from the sense of our faith and sanctification to justification, calling, predestination, and finally, foreknowledge of election. Once we have reached certainty about our election, we can descend gradually to ourselves, concluding the certainty of our perseverance and salvation, and savoring the sweet fruits of this assurance.

3. Carnal security, which may lead us to disregard the means of salvation due to our belief in the immutability of our election. This mistaken view ignores the importance of faith and holiness, which are integral to our journey of salvation (Ephesians 1:4; 2 Thessalonians 2:13; 1 Peter 1:2).

4. Desperation, wherein we conclude that we are not elect because we do not observe the marks of election in ourselves. Such despair can lead us to neglect faith, repentance, and godliness, which are essential. Instead, concern and desire for our election should drive us to hope, motivating us to pursue the means that ultimately lead to the certainty of our election.

5. Unnecessary doubts among true believers regarding their own election. These doubts hinder the intimacy between God and His chosen ones. While it is appropriate to humble ourselves and seek God's mercy after committing sins, we should not immediately abandon all hope and doubt our election to salvation due to individual weaknesses. Pointless doubts of this kind greatly hinder the close relationship between the elect and their God.

Reprobation

"Indeed, certain people have crept in unnoticed, who were once long ago marked out for this condemnation, ungodly people, who turn the grace of our God into lasciviousness and deny God, who is our only Master, and our Lord Jesus Christ." —Jude 4

The Transition to Reprobation

I. Just as election and reprobation are intricately connected, with each concept shedding light on the other, it is essential to grasp the significance of both. The existence of one implies the presence of the other; where there is election, reprobation also exists, and where there is no reprobation, there can be no genuine election. Therefore, a deeper understanding of one concept leads to a more profound comprehension of the other. With this in mind, let us transition from our exploration of election to an examination of reprobation, which the blessed apostle Jude illuminates in verse 4 of his epistle.

A. The Subject of Description: "For certain people have crept in unnoticed." The apostle identifies these as pseudo-Christians who, in terms of their outward profession, appear to be part of the Christian community. However, they have shamefully forsaken the Christian faith. These individuals, akin to the Simonians, Nicolaitans, Gnostics, Menandrites, Carpocratians, Cerinthians, Nazaraeans, Ebionites, and others mentioned by the apostle John as antichrists (1 John 2:18–19, 22; 4:1–3), propagated unorthodox teachings. Their doctrines included viewing sin as indifferent, advocating communal ownership of property, and more. This letter from Jude was written to address these false teachings, as confirmed by Oecumenius in his summary of the epistle. To describe their infiltration, Jude employs the phrase "crept in unnoticed," signifying that they entered the church in a clandestine and gradual manner.B. The Description Itself: The apostle outlines various aspects of their reprobation, represented by the phrase "who were once marked out beforehand for this judgment." This description encompasses the following elements:1. The Timing: "once," or "already," suggests that this reprobation was determined before their entrance into the church. In this context of eternal reprobation, "once" implies a timeless existence, similar to "from of old" or "from days of eternity" (Mic. 5:2).

2. The Act of Reprobation: The term "marked out beforehand" (προγεγραμμένοι) can be attributed to either Paul or Peter (2 Thess. 2:8–9; 2 Tim. 2:16; 2 Peter 2:3), or even to Christ Himself (Matt. 24:4–5, 10–11, 14). The purpose of this marking was to enable them to avoid eternal reprobation. Others connect it to Old Testament times, drawing from the practice of reciting written sentences, where those "destined" (1 Thess. 5:9), "prepared" (Rom. 9:22), and those "for whom the gloom of darkness has been reserved forever" (2 Peter 2:17) are portrayed. This points more fittingly toward eternal reprobation, supported by the idea of the "book of life" opposed to the "book of death." Furthermore, individuals often record their intentions in notebooks to ensure

they are accomplished, which aligns more accurately with the analogous descriptions of those "marked out beforehand" (1 Thess. 5:9; Rom. 9:22; 2 Peter 2:17) by eternal reprobation. This interpretation gains strength from the fact that Peter and Jude address the same individuals.

3. The Outcome: This marking out has a clear endpoint, represented as "for this very judgment" (εἰς τοῦτο τὸ κρίμα). "Judgment" (κρίμα) here may refer to the reprobate mindset that led them to distort the truth, the divine abandonment that allowed them to shipwreck their faith due to prior sins, or ultimately, eternal damnation. In this context, "judgment" is synonymous with "punishment" (as in Matt. 23:14; Mark 12:40; Luke 20:47; Rom. 2:3; 5:16; Gal. 5:10; James 3:1). God predetermined this punishment long ago for those who reject the gospel. Jude emphasizes that they were "marked out beforehand" (προγεγραμμένοι) for this eternal destruction, underscoring that it occurred not arbitrarily but as a result of God's eternal and just plan (2 Peter 2:22).

1. Ungodliness: ἀσεβεῖς, "ungodly people" (cf. 2 Peter 2:6). Ἀσεβής, derived from the root ἀ and σέβομαι, meaning "I worship," describes those who not only lack any inclination toward divine worship but also tend toward various sins. Consequently, ἀσεβεῖς, "the ungodly," and ἁμάρτωλοι, "sinners," are often mentioned together in the Scriptures (1 Tim. 1:9; 1 Peter 4:18; Jude 15). These terms are also associated with ἀπώλεια, "destruction" (2 Peter 3:7), and the wrath of God (Rom. 1:18; Jude 15). This is not because ungodliness is the primary cause of eternal reprobation but because it is a consequence of abandonment. It serves as a basis for their just condemnation, allowing the glory of avenging justice to be revealed in their rightful punishment.

2. The abuse and contempt of divine grace: τὴν τοῦ θεοῦ ἡμῶν χάριν μετατιθέντες εἰς ἀσέλγειαν, "who turn the grace of our God

into lasciviousness." In this reference to the misuse of grace, several aspects are evident:

a. The Starting Point: "the grace of our God." This phrase signifies the doctrine of grace or the gospel, often referred to metonymically, as seen in Hebrews 12:15 and other places. It encompasses the teaching of Christ's gracious redemption and our justification through faith alone. Jude emphasizes the significance of this grace by linking it to "our God" or the covenant of grace, wherein God becomes ours in Christ. This highlights the gravity of the abuse, as they pervert the grace associated with such a profound covenant.

b. The Act of Abusing: μετατιθέντες, meaning "those who turn" or transfer it, denotes diverting grace from its intended purpose to a corrupt one. The word is derived from the practice of moving belongings from one place to another (Acts 7:16; Heb. 7:12; 11:5). They distort it with perverse teachings, as also mentioned in Galatians 1:6.

c. The Endpoint: εἰς ἀσέλγειαν, "into lasciviousness," refers to shamelessness or impudence. It signifies the depravity that arises from excessive lust, as noted by Junius in Galatians 5:19. This term encompasses various forms of obscenity and lust, where inner desires manifest in shameless words and actions. It represents an extreme indulgence in all forms of lasciviousness, to which groups like the Simonians, Nicolaitans, Carpocratians, Gnostics, and others perverted the teachings concerning the grace of our God.

Apostasy: καὶ τὸν μόνον θεὸν καὶ δεσπότην, τὸν κύριον ἡμῶν Ἰησοῦν Χριστὸν ἀρνούμενοι, "and denying the only God and Master, our Lord Jesus Christ." This passage highlights the following:

a. Two objects of denial: i. The primary object: καὶ τὸν μόνον θεὸν καὶ δεσπότην, "and denying the only God and Master." Some interpret the three titles μόνον θεόν, "the only God," δεσπότην, "Master," and κύριον, "Lord," as referring to Jesus Christ alone, emphasizing that He, along with the Father, is the only God (John 17:3). He is also the Master or head of the household of the church and the Lord who redeemed us through His blood (1 Peter 1:18–19). The use of one article before the three titles is not uncommon when referring to distinct persons (Matt. 17:1; Acts 3:11). However, I prefer to understand the first two titles as referring to the Father. He is called: a) Μόνος θεός, "the only God," in contrast not only to created beings and false gods but also to the Son, to whom He is God in terms of the economy, as the Son voluntarily became a servant and subordinate to the Father (Isa. 53:10; John 20:17). b) Δεσπότης, "Master" or ruler (Luke 2:29; Acts 4:24). He is referred to as such because, in the context of the Trinity, He is the first person, just as the second person is the steward, and the third person is like their common emissary, as explained in the chapter on the Trinity. Additionally, He ordained the entire plan of redemption in the eternal counsel of peace and serves as the supreme Lawgiver within the church.

ii. The secondary object: τὸν κύριον ἡμῶν Ἰησοῦν Χριστόν, "our Lord Jesus Christ." Jesus Christ is frequently referred to as "Lord," not only due to His deity, through which He created, sustains, and governs all things, and His role in redemption, by which He purchased us for Himself (Rev. 5:9; 1 Cor. 6:20; 7:23), but also because He has been granted all authority by the Father (Matt. 28:18; Phil. 2:9–11; Acts 2:36).

b. The act of denying: ἀρνούμενοι, "denying." To deny someone is to strip away faith and authority from them (Matt. 10:33; Luke 12:9; Acts 3:13–14; 7:35). This denial is evident first in one's actions and way of life (Titus 1:16) and subsequently in one's words and teachings (Matt. 10:33). This term is used accurately in reference to groups like the Simonians, Nicolaitans, Carpocratians, and others, as previously discussed. These groups distorted the grace of God and denied, first, God the Father, by replacing the one true Governor of the world with several rulers, worshiping figures like Simon, who falsely claimed to be the God who appeared on Mount Sinai. They also denied Jesus Christ, asserting that He was not truly born, did not suffer, was not resurrected, and was not the Christ except in name. They believed in a different supreme, invisible, and incorporeal Christ, and rejected our Christ as a mere man born of man, equal to many of His followers. Consequently, they did not acknowledge Him as their Redeemer and Lord.

The Dogmatic Part

Proof of Eternal Reprobation

III. Thus, when we consider that it is specific individuals, not all, and these individuals are described by their distinct characteristics, who were not merely foreknown but predestined to a certain end—damnation—long ago, who can reasonably doubt the existence of an eternal decree through which God intended to reveal the glory of His avenging justice?

Supported by Scripture

This truth is reinforced by Scripture in numerous ways, both explicitly and implicitly. The Scriptures explicitly state, "I have chosen you; I have not rejected you" (Isaiah 51:9). Implication also underscores the concept when we read that certain individuals are prepared for destruction (Romans 9:22), appointed (1 Peter 2:8–9, "...to which they were also appointed. But you are a chosen race"), hated by God (Romans 9:9, 11–13; Malachi 1:2–3; Romans 11:15). Moreover, Scripture informs us that God has mercy on whom He wills and hardens whom He wills, and there are those whose names are not found in the book of life (Revelation 13:8). These passages make it clear that some are not among the people of God and are not beloved (Hosea 1:10; 2:23; cf. Romans 9:25).

Reason Supports the Notion

IV. Furthermore, reason itself substantiates this understanding. (1) If there is election, a concept widely accepted, then logically, there is also reprobation; it follows naturally from the relationship between the two. (2) Reason dictates that due to God's perfection, nothing occurs in time that He did not foresee from eternity. His foreknowledge must stem from His predetermination. Consequently, if He foresaw the damnation of many, it is necessary that He predetermined it from eternity—this is reprobation. Moreover, (3) since God has had a unique care for the state of rational, eternal creatures from eternity in predestination, He must have had such care for their damnation in reprobation as well. (4) Given that He had care for some in electing them, it is a logical necessity that He passed over others, leaving them in their sins and eternally damned. And finally, (5) it is fitting to believe that God has taken care from eternity to demonstrate both His avenging justice and His grace and mercy.

What Reprobation Entails

V. Reprobation can be understood as the predestination of specific individuals, chosen for their just condemnation, with the purpose of manifesting the glory of God's avenging justice (Romans 9:22; Jude 4). When we refer to it as predestination (as discussed in the chapter on predestination), we do not mean mere and ineffective foreknowledge. Instead, it signifies a deliberate act of God's will, where He hardens, positions, fits, and prescribes certain individuals for their ultimate destruction. This predestination is not a general decree related to the state of unbelievers and the ungodly, as it always pertains to specific individuals—referred to as "certain people" or "vessels of wrath." Nor is it a vague predestination but one that focuses on definite persons, such as Esau. Furthermore, this predestination aims to reveal the glory of God's justice, not the damnation of humanity as an end in itself. God does not delight in the death of sinners for its own sake, as evident from passages like Ezekiel 18:23. The distinction between election and reprobation lies in their ends: while election seeks both the glory of mercy and the salvation of the elect (Romans 9:23), reprobation aims solely to manifest justice and considers the just condemnation of the reprobate only as a means.

The Four Aspects of Reprobation

VI. The predestination of reprobation encompasses four facets: (1) The purpose of revealing the glory of God's avenging justice (Romans 9:22). It does not seek the damnation or destruction of humanity as a good end in itself, for such an end cannot be considered good, neither in the eyes of God nor humans. God declares that He does not take pleasure in the death of sinners (Ezekiel 18:23). In contrast, election has a dual end: the glory of mercy and the salvation of the elect (Romans 9:23). (2) The purpose of creating and permitting the fall, shared by the reprobate and elect alike, so that none, including Cain and Judas, has a valid complaint. God's purpose here is to glorify His justice through the creation of humankind, their general existence, and the permission of their fall—a matter that does not inflict harm on anyone, especially as reprobation is an immanent act of God and does not affect anyone directly. (3) The designation of specific individuals, like Judas, from the fallen, with the goal of manifesting God's justice. This act cannot be considered election, as it lacks love and the communication of any good; rather, it signifies the privation of both. This aspect constitutes reprobation in its strictest sense because it involves the rejection and separation of individuals from God's love—unlike election, which involves love and separation. This is what is called the negative hatred of reprobation, which is accompanied by positive hatred. In positive hatred, God wills certain individuals to be deprived of eternal life and justly condemned for their sins (Romans 9:13). (4) The intention to prepare and direct the means through which justice can be manifested in the reprobate. The primary means for this purpose are the permission of sin, abandonment in sin (Romans 9:18; 2 Thessalonians 2:11–12), and just condemnation due to sin. Here lies another distinction between election and reprobation: election is the cause not only of salvation but also of all its means, whereas reprobation is not properly the cause of damnation or the sin that merits damnation but only the antecedent cause. Additionally, reprobation means do not have a cause-and-effect relationship among themselves, while election means do (calling causes justification, and justification causes glorification). It's worth noting that reprobation means are predominantly negative, such as non-redemption (John 10:26), non-calling, non-effectual calling, non-bestowing of faith (Acts 13:48; John 12:39–40), non-obstruction of sin, abandonment in sin (Romans 9:18), and non-remission of sin (John 20:23). Nonetheless, there are also positive means, including blinding, hardening (Isaiah 6:9; John 12:39–40), and just condemnation due to sin (John 12:39–40; Romans 9:22; Jude 4). All these means, whether negative or positive, are directed toward their end through a positive act of God's will.

The Scope of Reprobation

VII. We have already established that humanity can be the object of divine reprobation in various stages of existence: as potentially creatable and fallible, as about to be created and about to fall, as created and fallen, and as rejected or reprobate. It is essential to note that reprobation is not limited to adults but extends to infants, even those who pass away in their infancy. While the infants of believers are under the promise of the covenant of grace and considered holy (Genesis 17:7; Acts 2:39), the children of unbelievers are regarded as impure. They were formerly excluded from the covenant due to their uncircumcision and, through original sin, are susceptible to damnation and even more so to reprobation (Romans 5:14). However, whether all infants of unbelievers who die in infancy are indeed reprobated is a matter left to God's determination in due time.

The Divine Cause of Reprobation and Its Motivation

VIII. It is crucial to recognize that while sin renders an individual liable to damnation and deserving of it due to the just punishment that corresponds to culpable wrongdoing, sin does not render someone subject to reprobation. The ability of God to choose, from among those equally fallen, one person over another for the purpose of manifesting His justice does not result from sin. Instead, it stems from the absolute sovereignty of God (Romans 9:21; Matthew 20:15). Sin may serve as the meritorious cause of the eternal punishment appointed for the reprobate, but it does not cause the act of predestination itself (Romans 9:11–12, 19). This act of predestination is independent, eternal, and a product of God's own decree. Thus, there exists no principal cause of reprobation other than God (Romans 9:11–12, 19; Jeremiah 6:30), and no driving force apart from His good pleasure (Romans 9:18–21; Matthew 11:25–26). Any conceivable cause—such as sin, unbelief, impiety, or impenitence—follows reprobation and cannot have been a pre-existing or foreseen cause for it. God's foresight is subsequent to His decree. The primary and direct purpose of reprobation is the display of His authority and justice or wrath (Romans 9:23), while its indirect purpose or collateral effect is the illumination of His grace and mercy toward the elect (Romans 9:22–23).

The Unconditional Nature of Reprobation

IX. Reprobation is absolutely unconditional. This means that while it does not entirely exclude consideration of sin within the divine decree, it does so only in certain respects. Sin is included in the second act of reprobation, which decrees the permission of sin, enabling God to reveal His avenging justice. Sin is also presupposed in the third act, as God, among the sinful, reprobates whom He wills. Lastly, sin is included in the fourth act because just damnation, by its nature, presupposes sin and views it as the meritorious cause. However, sin is not considered the driving or meritorious cause for which God decrees the manifestation of His avenging justice or for which He selects one person for reprobation over another (Romans 9:11, 13). To suggest otherwise would imply a dependence of God's decree on His creatures, rendering the creature independent.

The Immutable and Certain Nature of Reprobation

X. Reprobation, as with any divine decree, is immutable. This immutability arises from the unchanging nature of God Himself, with whom the act of reprobation coincides. God remains eternally constant (Psalm 102:26–27; Hebrews 1:11–12; Malachi 3:6). Furthermore, reprobation is unalterable on the part of the reprobate. Those who do not believe in the Son will not attain life, and the wrath of God will persist upon them (John 3:36). Consequently, the number of the reprobate is certain and definite, known exclusively to God (Romans 9:11–12). This encompasses not just the abstract number or quantity but also the concrete number or the specific individuals destined for damnation. As Scripture attests, "Esau I have hated" (Romans 9:13). This certainty is evident from the analogy with election (Romans 8:29–30; 2 Timothy 2:19) and will be fully realized in the execution of reprobation on the last day (Matthew 25:32).

The Elenctic Part: Addressing Key Questions

XI. Many of the disputes in this chapter find their resolutions in the concepts we have previously established in the three preceding chapters. Nevertheless, it is worthwhile to provide a concise overview of these questions. Thus, we inquire first whether there exists a specific, personal reprobation ordained by God from eternity. The Socinians and other proponents of an independent, indifferent free choice acknowledge a reprobation of state, determined from eternity, in which God rejects those who persist as unbelievers and ungodly until their deaths. They also acknowledge a reprobation of individuals, but one that is not eternal, occurring only at the moment of the sinner's death. They hold this view primarily because they deny God foreknowledge of future contingencies and desire a free choice that remains self-determined until death. On the other hand, the semi-Pelagians of Marseille, joined by the Jesuits, Anabaptists, Lutherans, and Remonstrants, allow a personal reprobation determined from eternity, but not an absolute and irrevocable one, as they, like the Socinians, place it at the moment of death.

Supporting Arguments

In contrast, the Reformed position, in alignment with Scripture, upholds only a personal reprobation determined from eternity, absolutely and irrevocably. There are several reasons for this stance. (1) Scripture asserts that God hated Esau before he had performed any good or evil (Romans 9:13), and it describes the vessels of wrath as prepared for destruction (Romans 9:22), established (1 Peter 2:8), foreordained (Jude 4), and created for the day of evil (Proverbs 16:4). (2) As previously demonstrated, every decree of God, including all aspects of predestination and election, is independent, eternal, absolute, and immutable. Therefore, reprobation follows the same pattern.

Addressing Objections with Pastoral Care

Objections and Responses:

Our adversaries raise various objections against our position, but once we have established the eternal and infallible foreknowledge of God concerning future contingencies and explained the nature of free choice, their accusations mostly insult not our teaching, but rather the very character of God. These objections include:

1. Reprobation deprives sinners of their freedom and forces them into sin. In response: (a) Reprobation, as an immanent act of God, does not diminish human liberty. (b) It does not hinder sinners from freely choosing to sin through counsel and deliberation. God ordained reprobation so that sinners would sin freely. (c) True necessity arises only from a cause that inherently leads to an effect, which reprobation does not imply.

2. Reprobation makes God the author of all sin. In response: (a) Reprobation does not make sinners sin necessarily or according to their nature. (b) God predestined individuals not to sin but to demonstrate His avenging justice through just condemnation. (c) The author of sin is the one who commits it, which is contrary to God's nature.

3. Reprobation makes God unjust, punishing sinners who, due to the irrevocable decree, cannot avoid sin. In response: (a) Sinners can still avoid sin in terms of their ability, as the decree does not necessitate them to sin. (b) God condemns based on sin and only decrees damnation due to sin. (c) Reprobation itself is an act of authority and sovereignty.

4. Reprobation makes God appear cruel by predestining creatures to eternal condemnation purely based on His good pleasure before they even existed or sinned. In response: (a) Scripture speaks in this manner (Romans 9:22; Jude 4; 1 Thessalonians 5:9; 2 Peter 2:8–9; Malachi 1:2–3; Romans 9:11–13). (b) God does not destine to eternal damnation but to demonstrate His avenging justice through just condemnation. (c) Reprobation, as an immanent act, does not harm or condemn the creature or delight in their death unless they remain impenitent (Proverbs 1:25–27).

5. Reprobation might make God appear hypocritical for calling individuals to repentance and life while also predestining them to unrepentance and death. In response, God earnestly calls to repentance and promises life when it is present, even if He did not decree to bring about repentance in a person, as He is not obligated to do so by any right.

6. Reprobation seems to show partiality, as it designates unequal fates to equal individuals. In response, God owes no creature anything, and He designates unequal fates not to equals but to unequals, believers and unbelievers.

7. Reprobation supposedly gives wicked individuals a just reason to complain that God did not elect them. In response: (a) God is not obligated to elect anyone, as He is the absolute Lord of

all. (b) These complaints would only be valid if the wicked were unjustly hindered from performing good deeds, which is not the case; they freely and joyfully choose to sin.

8. Reprobation is believed to hinder comfort and godliness by causing people to fear they are reprobate. In response: (a) No one can be certain of their reprobation, though the ungodly can be sure they are outside of grace. (b) Such fear can lead to repentance. (c) It encourages godly individuals to work out their salvation with fear and trembling and make their election and calling sure through good works. Ultimately, it provides comfort when one realizes they are part of God's chosen few.

With the truth of our doctrine of reprobation firmly established, we confront these objections with the Pauline response: "But who are you, O man, to respond against God? Will the pot say to the potter, 'Why have you made me like this?' Does not the potter have authority over the clay, to make from the same lump a vessel for honor and a vessel for dishonor?" (Romans 9:20–21).

Divine Will and Sin as Causes of Reprobation

1. Is it an act of the divine intellect only, or also of the divine will?

We ponder, secondly, whether reprobation stems solely from the divine intellect or encompasses the divine will as well. Should we describe the reprobate as merely foreknown rather than predestined? Is reprobation a distinct part or category within predestination? These intertwined questions have been previously addressed in our third book, chapter 2, §XXIV. We bring them forth here to consider the contentions surrounding reprobation.

1. Is sin the impelling cause of reprobation? The difference of opinions

As our third question, we inquire whether sin serves as the meritorious or in some way, the impelling cause of reprobation. The Pelagians, Socinians, semi-Pelagians, Jesuits, Remonstrants, Lutherans, and those beyond the Reformed Church concur that their general reprobation, which pertains to a state ("I will to condemn all unbelievers and impenitent individuals"), relies solely on the divine good pleasure, as it does not disrupt the independent indifference of free choice. However, they all link personal reprobation to sin as its impelling cause.

The View of the Reformed with Their Reasons

The Reformed perspective distinguishes between damnation, for which they acknowledge sin, unbelief, and other factors as the meritorious causes, and reprobation. They do admit that reprobation takes into account sin, even considering all its facets: the first act ("I will to declare the glory of my avenging justice in the just damnation of sinners") presupposes the possibility of sin; the second ("I will to create men and permit their fall") envisions the future occurrence of sin; the third ("I will to separate, for example, Esau and Judas, from among the created and fallen, that in their just condemnation, I may manifest my justice") incorporates sin as the meritorious cause of condemnation; and the fourth ("I will to leave, for instance, Cain, Ham, Esau, Judas in their sins, not to redeem them, not to grant them faith, but to condemn them on account of sin, so that in this just condemnation, I may display the glory of my avenging justice") encompasses sin along with condemnation as the means to showcase His avenging justice. However, sin is not included as the impelling cause of the act of reprobation itself. This is because:

1. Scripture attributes the act of reprobation solely to the unadulterated good pleasure of God (Rom. 9:11, 18, 21; Matt. 11:25–26; 10:15; Ps. 115:3).

2. Sin is not the cause of the eternal will, while the act of reprobation consists entirely of the will of God (Rom. 9:18). The

decreeing will of God serves as the primary and supreme cause of all future events, and it does not rely on anything higher. Furthermore, a timeless existence cannot be influenced by a cause that exists only within time, as it would imply an effect preceding its own cause.

3. If sin were the cause of reprobation, all humanity would be reprobate, given that all people, by nature, are sinners (Eph. 2:3).

4. Scripture indicates that God created the wicked for the evil day (Prov. 16:4).

5. It is stated that God hardens those whom He wills (Rom. 9:18).

6. Reprobation is nothing other than the act of God who reprobates, as we previously explained in the chapter on divine decrees.

7. The future occurrence of sin can only be foreseen through the divine decree, as the futurity of anything can be traced back to nothing else but the decree itself.

8. According to the opposing view, the act of reprobation would be contingent upon human sin, whether the individuals were already created or yet to be created.

Objections

It is not valid to argue to the contrary:

1. Claiming that the perdition of the reprobate is solely due to sin, and that perdition is essentially reprobation (Hos. 13:9). In response, this argument is flawed because reprobation has existed from eternity, while perdition occurs in time. That which exists in time cannot be the same as that which has existed from

eternity.

2. Asserting that sin alone is the reason people will be damned at the last judgment (Matt. 25:41ff.). In reply, damnation is fundamentally different from reprobation, as the eternal differs from the temporary.

3. Stating that sin alone is the cause of divine hatred (Ps. 5:4–6), and yet God's hatred is the cause of reprobation (Rom. 9:13). The response is that God's hatred is reprobation itself, not the cause of reprobation (Rom. 9:13). Additionally, the term "hatred" can sometimes refer to punishment (Ps. 5:4–6), the cause of which is unquestionably sin. However, sin is not the cause of reprobation itself, which precedes punishment.

4. Contending that if God, based solely on His good pleasure, reprobates so many people, He cannot be considered good, but rather a tyrant and an unjust judge. In reply, this assertion is incorrect because God, through reprobation, has not chosen to damn anyone except on account of sin as the meritorious cause of damnation. Our adversaries themselves acknowledge that there is no valid argument for malice or injustice in this regard.

Is a Person Predestined to Sin or Destruction?

It is asked, fourthly, whether the end of reprobation is either the sin of the reprobate, their condemnation, or their destruction, or whether a person is predestined by God to sin or condemnation. In response, the affirmative view is imposed upon the Reformed through a false accusation. From their perspective, sin is neither intended by God as the end nor as the means, although the just punishment of sin is included in the divine decree, not as its ultimate end, but as a means. With us, the end of reprobation is solely the manifestation of God's avenging justice through the just condemnation of the sinner, along with the manifestation of His absolute authority. This aligns with the language of Scripture (Rom. 9:17, 21; Matt. 20:15). God did not create individuals as reprobate or permit sin with the intention of damning them. Instead, creation, permission of sin, and abandonment in sin represent a unified means aiming to achieve the ultimate end: the manifestation of God's authority and avenging justice as His supreme purpose, as we have previously demonstrated.

Is Man Not Only as Fallen but Also as Unbelieving the Object of Reprobation?

Fifthly, it is asked whether the object of reprobation includes not only fallen and sinful man but also an unbeliever, and consequently, whether infants can be subject to reprobation. The Pelagians and Socinians, believing that the human will remains unchangeable throughout life, regardless of any divine decree, make the object of personal and absolute reprobation someone who is, in reality, an unbeliever. Additionally, due to their denial of original sin, they completely exclude infants from reprobation.

The semi-Pelagians, acknowledging divine foreknowledge and attributing foreseen unbelief as the impelling cause of reprobation, consider adults who will not believe in reality as the objects of reprobation. However, when it comes to infants, while they dare not assert their entry into heaven based on 1 Corinthians 7:14, they do not recognize reprobation for them. Instead, they assign them to a certain intermediate state, involving only the punishment of loss, similar to their stance on pagans dying in their persistent unbelief.

The Lutherans, asserting that every person has been redeemed and will be called, commanding all to believe, believe that the object of reprobation comprises those who will genuinely not believe. As for infants, they do not provide any specific doctrine that I am aware of.

The Reformed position is that the object of reprobation, in a broader sense as it relates to predestination, signifies the purpose of manifesting the glory of avenging justice, which includes man's ability to be created and to fall. However, in a stricter sense, when discussing segregation, the object is fallen man who is a sinner. Yet, the Reformed do not find in Scripture the precise notion that man as an unbeliever is the object of reprobation, except possibly in the context of the final act that decrees the just condemnation of the reprobate and with regard to specific individuals who rejected Christ when offered to them.

Scripture also identifies those not yet born and who have not done either good or evil as objects of reprobation, considering unbelief as a consequence of reprobation (Matt. 13:11–15; John 12:37–40; Matt. 11:25–26). Therefore, they maintain that certain infants can be subject to reprobation since they are susceptible to original sin (Rom. 5:12, 14), are considered unholy and impure (1 Cor. 7:14), and are outside the covenant of grace (Gen. 17:7–8; Acts 2:39).

Regarding the infants of believers, as they are regarded as pure (1 Cor. 7:14) and within the covenant (Acts 2:39; Gen. 17:7) and are considered partakers of their parents' faith, the Reformed hold a more positive view. However, concerning the infants of unbelievers, where Scripture provides no explicit determination, they believe the matter should be left to divine judgment. Given that we have already presented the Reformed hypotheses extensively in this matter in the preceding sections, and considering that our adversaries lack anything other than their own hypotheses, which we have also refuted, we deem it unnecessary to add further to these arguments.

Is Reprobation Absolute?

Sixthly, the question arises: Is the reprobation of specific individuals from eternity absolute, or does it depend on the condition of final unbelief? Our adversaries assert that the reprobation of one's state, as well as the peremptory reprobation of individuals occurring at the moment of death, is absolute. However, they argue that personal reprobation, made from eternity, is contingent upon the voluntary unbelief of the individual.

In contrast, the Reformed, in harmony with the teachings of Scripture, embrace reprobation not in terms of one's state but specifically concerning individuals. They believe it to be eternal and absolute, with the just condemnation of the sinner being contingent upon sin and unbelief, but they find no scriptural basis for suggesting that reprobation itself depends on these conditions. Indeed, according to the nature of every divine decree, they maintain that reprobation is entirely independent, eternal, and absolute, as we have previously demonstrated in the chapter on the decree.

Is Reprobation Immutable?

Seventhly, we inquire whether reprobation is certain and immutable. Our Pelagianizing adversaries contend that reprobation of one's state and peremptory reprobation at the moment of death are immutable. However, they argue that non-peremptory reprobation, which is contingent upon voluntary unbelief, can be altered according to human choice.

The Lutherans, like in the matter of election, also seem to make distinctions regarding reprobation. They suggest that with regard to divine foreknowledge, reprobation must be considered immutable, but concerning humans, it can change so that someone may transition from being reprobate to becoming elect, and vice versa.

On the other hand, the Reformed, guided by Scripture (Rom. 11:7), by the analogy of election, and by the nature of every divine decree, firmly believe that the decree of reprobation is entirely immutable and unchangeable. Their adversaries have nothing substantial to support their position except divine promises, through which God pledges to withhold judgment for the penitent among the wicked (e.g., Jer. 18:7–8). However, it is important to note that divine promises differ significantly from divine decrees, as we have explained elsewhere, in the chapter on the will of God.

As for the calumnies and accusations of our adversaries, particularly concerning this aspect of our doctrine of reprobation, claiming that it undermines human free will and the contingency of events, imposes a fatalistic and Stoic necessity upon all things, attributes the authorship of sin to God, portrays Him as an unjust deceiver and pretender, and eradicates all fervor for religion and godliness—these allegations have been adequately addressed in §XI of this chapter.

The Practical Implications

The contemplation of reprobation serves as a profound reflection on the glory of God, which is His primary purpose in this divine counsel (Rom. 9:22–23). In considering reprobation, we must understand that, just as in election, God's chief aim is His own glory and the salvation of humanity. He could not have intended the destruction or damnation of mankind as an end in itself because, inherently, it possesses no inherent goodness. Instead, reprobation vividly demonstrates the glory:

1. Of His absolute divine authority and sovereignty — "willing to make His power known" (Rom. 9:22). God exercises His authority as a potter, shaping vessels of mercy and vessels of wrath or justice from the same lump of clay. He acts according to His pure and unadulterated good pleasure, selecting some for reprobation while leaving others unchosen, such as Ishmael and Esau. He does so without conferring upon them the means of grace, hardening their hearts, abandoning them to their sinful ways, and ultimately justly condemning them because of their transgressions. This underscores God's supreme authority and power, which we have explored further in previous chapters on predestination and the authority of God.

2. Of His wrath, severity, and avenging justice — "willing to show

His wrath" (Rom. 9:22). This contemplation reveals the severity with which God has excluded sinners from His grace and the means of salvation, condemning them to eternal punishment due to their sins. It is as though God proclaims, "For this very purpose I have raised you up, that I may show my power in you, and that my name may be declared" (Rom. 9:17). We must acknowledge both the kindness and severity of God (Rom. 11:22).

Divine Wisdom

Moreover, it reveals the glory of God's wisdom (3), as He, in His infinite wisdom, skillfully employs means to manifest His wrath and justice without compromising His goodness. Astonishingly, He turns even the gravest evil, sin, into a means to showcase the highest good, which is the glory of His avenging justice. In contemplating this, we must humbly exclaim, "Oh the riches of the wisdom and knowledge of God! How inscrutable are His judgments! And His ways past finding out! Who has known the mind of the Lord? Or who has been His counselor?" (Rom. 11:33–34). The doctrine of reprobation highlights God's power, severe justice, and infinite wisdom so profoundly that we are not only called to acknowledge and consider it but also to:

1. Submit ourselves and all things to His authority, humbly recognizing our finite understanding and yielding to His divine sovereignty. We should refrain from challenging God's wisdom and purposes and instead reflect on our own limitations. As the Scriptures remind us, "But who are you, O man, to respond against God? Will the pot say to the potter, 'Why have you made me like this?'" (Rom. 9:20).

2. Approach His avenging justice with reverence and awe, recognizing the severity of His judgments. We should not be haughty but fear His righteous judgments (Rom. 11:20).

3. Embrace His inscrutable wisdom, setting aside our human reasoning, especially in matters related to reprobation. We should humble ourselves and acknowledge that our understanding is limited. Instead of relying on our own understanding, we should place our trust in the wisdom of God and remain silent, saying, "Because you, O Lord, have done it" (Ps. 39:9) and "It is Jehovah. Let Him do what is good in His eyes" (1 Sam. 3:18).

4. It cautions us against accusing God

In light of reprobation, we must also heed a warning:

1. Beware, more than one would fear a dog or a snake, of allowing our own fleshly reasoning to align with the enemies of truth in defense of the reprobate. We must avoid positioning ourselves as their advocates, contending against God, the supreme judge. It is utterly sinful and wicked to challenge the Almighty on behalf of man and to act as accusers and judges. Such actions involve accusing God of various offenses, such as injustice, cruelty, respect of persons, hypocrisy, being the author of sin, and providing an argument for the wicked to complain and excuse themselves. It also leads to despair for the miserable, as they feel constrained by the harsh fate of reprobation. We should guard against these carnal accusations more diligently than we would guard against a dangerous animal. Not only is it deeply sinful and wicked to contend with the great and good God on behalf of humanity, but it is also blasphemous to suspect God of such grave iniquity. Additionally, it is self-destructive for individuals to engage in disputes with their Creator (Gen. 18:27; Job 9:2–4).

2. Instead, we should boldly stand up for God, not only against the misguided thoughts of our own minds but also against

the accusations of adversaries. We should vigorously refute the accusations we mentioned earlier using sound reasoning and similar arguments, as we have already done against individual adversaries in a previous section. We must find solace in the fact that God has not reprobated us, drawing confidence from the fact that we have not been cast aside by Him. We demonstrate our loyalty to Him and His glory by defending His righteousness, both against our own doubts and the insults of those who disparage Him (Matt. 12:30; cf. Rom. 8:31).

3. It magnifies the splendor of divine mercy. Toward whom?

XX. Furthermore, thirdly, reprobation unveils the profound glory of divine mercy, initially directed even towards the reprobate themselves. God not only shows remarkable restraint in His patience toward the vessels of wrath destined for destruction (Rom. 9:22), but He frequently lavishes them with numerous and extraordinary earthly blessings, sometimes even exceeding those bestowed upon the elect (Pss. 17:14; 73:3, 12). What's more, He graces them with spiritual blessings of the highest order, nearly approaching salvation (Heb. 6:4–5), despite having the authority to withhold all grace and consign them to eternal damnation (Lam. 3:22; Isa. 1:9). Additionally, it vividly demonstrates divine mercy's glory, particularly toward the elect: "Willing to show his wrath, he endured vessels of wrath prepared for destruction, so that he might make known the riches of his glory toward vessels of his mercy, which he prepared beforehand for glory" (Rom. 9:22–23). This is because (1) God, in His absolute sovereignty, could have chosen to reprobate the elect just as He did with the reprobate, as "Who has first given to him that it might be repaid to him?" (Rom. 11:35). (2) The elect, too, were fallen, capable of being reprobated, and naturally children of wrath (Eph. 2:1, 3). Consequently, (3) they possessed no inherent superiority over the reprobate that would render them less deserving of reprobation (Ezek.

16:3-7). Finally, (4) nothing other than God's pure and unadulterated good pleasure (Luke 12:32; Eph. 1:5) can account for why He chose us to be vessels of mercy destined for glory over them.

And for what purpose?

Hence, from these considerations, we find compelling reasons why we should:

1. Humbly present ourselves in gratitude to God (Matt. 11:25; Eph. 1:3-4).

2. Love God more profoundly in response (Ps. 116:1, 8, 16).

3. Renounce all worldly pursuits for His sake (Ps. 73:25-26; Heb. 11:24-26; Phil. 3:7-8).

4. Recognize our distinction as vessels of grace, prepared for His glory, set apart from the reprobate (Rom. 9:23; Eph. 1:6; 2 Tim. 2:21).

5. Embrace humility and modesty, avoiding arrogance towards the reprobate, and instead, extending mercy towards them (1 Cor. 4:7; Rom. 11:18).

6. Approach our salvation with vigilance and awe, diligently working out our own salvation with fear and trembling, mindful that it is God who empowers us both to will and to do (Phil. 2:12; Rom. 11:20; Ps. 2:11).

7. It cautions us against harboring the belief of our own or others' reprobation

XXI. Consequently, fourthly, in order to fulfill these recommendations more diligently, let us exercise the utmost caution in imagining or, even more perilously, persuading ourselves of either our own or others' reprobation. Although certain individuals, including the apostles, were convinced of the reprobation of specific individuals through extraordinary revelations supplemented by external signs (1 Peter 2:8; Jude 4), and while ordinary indicators might legitimately lead you to doubt or be certain that you or someone else currently stands outside the realm of grace and would face condemnation if they were to die, it remains that no one can be absolutely certain that they will never experience God's conversion. Consequently, no one can be certain of their own reprobation. The very sins that might lead one to assume reprobation could also occur in the elect (1 Tim. 1:13–14; Matt. 26:72), with the exception of the sin of blaspheming the Holy Spirit, which the apostle declares as irredeemable (Heb. 6:4, 6). However, since it is difficult to be certain, at least easily, that one has committed this sin, the elect must be cautious never to entertain doubts or, more significantly, the conviction of their own reprobation. Doing so: (1) has the potential to extinguish love for God, intimacy with Him, confidence and tranquility in His presence, the courage to approach Him in prayer, zeal for repentance and piety, and the entire vitality of one's faith (1 John 4:18). Furthermore, (2) it is prone to rob individuals of all joy in God, inner peace, and, consequently, the vitality and sweetness of their Christian life, replacing it with a life marked by sorrow and a sense of spiritual deadness. Similarly, one should never entertain suspicions, let alone convictions, regarding a neighbor's reprobation, no matter how wicked their current conduct may be. For God retains the ability to effect their conversion (Rom. 11:23) and has not disclosed His intention to anyone. If you entertain even a suspicion or conviction of your neighbor's reprobation by God, you effectively close off any path to their improvement (1 John 5:16). Hence, it is better to employ the phrase coined by the apostle Paul, "We are confident of better things concerning you" (Heb. 6:9).

> 1. Let us diligently cultivate our own salvation with reverence and vigilance, guarding against the vices associated with the reprobate

XXII. Simultaneously, fifthly, let the severity of reprobation drive us to earnestly pursue our own salvation with reverence and vigilance (Phil. 2:12). We must not become haughty but maintain a healthy fear (Rom. 11:20, 22; Ps. 2:11; 1 Cor. 10:12). As the elect, we must be cautious not to fall into the vices that characterize the reprobate, as indulging in such behaviors could cast suspicion of reprobation upon ourselves or others. Take heed of these vices, exemplified by Jude in verse 4: (1) hypocrisy, which involves entering the church with a false display of faith and counterfeit piety; (2) the misuse of divine grace and a false sense of security, leading to licentiousness (Rom. 3:8); (3) apostasy, where one denies God as the only Master and Jesus Christ as our Lord; (4) taking offense at Christ and the truth of His Word, making oneself disobedient to Him (1 Peter 2:8); (5) engaging in sins that could lead to the sin particular to the reprobate, blasphemy against the Holy Spirit. Such sins include (a) grieving the Holy Spirit, by whom we were sealed (Eph. 4:30); (b) provoking Him (Isa. 63:10); (c) resisting Him (Acts 7:51–52); (d) quenching Him (1 Thess. 5:19). Beyond this, (e) the next step is blasphemy against the Holy Spirit (Matt. 12:31–32), a clear indication of reprobation. Lastly, (6) be aware of any sins that characterized notable reprobates like Cain, Saul, Judas, and others.

1. Conversely, let us focus on the virtues that distinctly set us apart from the reprobate

XXIII. Conversely, sixthly, recognizing that we are not mere vessels of wood or clay destined for dishonor, but rather vessels of gold and silver fashioned for honor (2 Tim. 2:20), prepared in advance for glory (Rom. 9:23), let us wholeheartedly embrace the virtues that distinguish the elect from the reprobate. The apostle provides a sample of these virtues in 2 Timothy 2:19, 21: (1) forsaking all unrighteousness; (2) cleansing ourselves of sins to become vessels of honor; (3) preparing ourselves for the Lord's purposes; (4) equipping ourselves for every good work;

(5) striving to be holy and blameless in the sight of God through love (Eph. 1:4); (6) as the elect, clothing ourselves with compassion, kindness, humility, gentleness, patience, and love (Col. 3:12–14); (7) practicing obedience (1 Peter 1:2); (8) defending evangelical truth (Phil. 4:3), and many other virtues of this nature that are particularly distinct from the vices of the reprobate.

www.ingramcontent.com/pod-product-compliance
Lightning Source LLC
Chambersburg PA
CBHW051319120626
46547CB00015B/2306

*9 7 8 1 9 6 1 8 0 7 3 8 9 *